The Great Lak

Edited by Walter B

2013, Felix Exi, Traverse City, MI

Thanks to Melissa for making sure that this book was more than a cluttered file on my computer.

Thanks to Eric for his generosity in Sturgeon Bay.

And, lastly, thanks to all the authors who shared their stories.

Contents

Contents

Preface

The purpose of this book was initially to respect the lakes and their ubiquitous presence in so many peoples' lives: something simple to understand, something that I could easily wrap my mind around and figured many people would probably enjoy reading about. I posted a few ads on websites calling for submissions, I e-mailed some acquaintances, and, admittedly a bit half-heartedly, I began work on what is now The Great Lakes Book Project. The name has always been the same, but before, the emphasis was on "The Great Lakes," whereas now, it is surely more on "Project." This is not to say that the lakes have lost importance, but instead, that while previously the project was a vehicle for The Great Lakes, now The Great Lakes are a vehicle for the project. What I saw from the very beginning was that, amongst all the different authors who submitted to the project, while the stories and locations were rarely the same, an overbearing theme was strikingly conspicuous.

In almost every piece, the lakes (or maybe just the region itself) were more than something beautiful or awesome or terrifying. Instead of a pretty picture, they were a sublime and abstract projection of what each author desired: something that, during times of strife or turmoil, could be pulled away from whatever safe spot the memory had been nestled away to, a skeleton for structure and strength that would always exist in one's cerebral background. When I read these, I understood that I felt the same things in the lakes. Unknowingly, I think that's why I was drawn to the idea of the project. I read these and I understood what they meant, and to be able to relate on such a personal and hidden level was rewarding. The world is full of detachment—since we are too busy to talk in person, we use the phone. Since we are too busy to use the phone, we text. Since we are too busy to text, we use half-words and little, horrible, grinning yellow faces and symbols that stain the screens and the eyes and the minds that see them, and somewhere along the line a lot of us forgot what it is like to relate to someone. This book is a testament to those who still want so badly for empathy and solidarity to exist.

I was lucky enough to meet several of the authors and interview them for a promotional video created to help market the book. At first, I was nervous. Even the most boisterous and bold must admit that walking into one's world and professional realm can be a bit intimidating, but, beyond the few awkward salutations where I was unsure whether to refer to the author by his or her first name or the prestigious "Dr." engraved before it on the placard glued to the wood frame office door, the interviews were fluid and enjoyable. So much that it was unnerving. Not to say that I expected tribulation, but I certainly didn't not expect it either. What happened when these amazing people spoke to me about their lives, fears, and memories was that I realized we all felt the same about the lakes. Not on an exact and specific level, but that, when life became stressful and tenuous, immune to our troubles, there would still be the lakes. To realize that was as rewarding as anything I've ever experienced.

I grew up, like almost everyone it seems, in a jaded generation—one filled with people who were so assured of their uniqueness and immense worth that they couldn't possibly be bothered with the idea that someone out there felt the same way. This project changed that for me. Not all the pieces are about this, but what they are about is an exposure of certain emotions and feelings, maybe certain emotions and feelings that you will find familiar. That's why I wanted to make this book: because I have felt what it is like to relate to someone on something that is important to me. I have felt what it is like to know that, even in my most secret thoughts, I am not alone and, direly, I want to share that feeling with as many people as I can.

Wolf Hunt

Steve Dudas

The Keweenaw claws its way out of the Upper Peninsula's northern coast and into a cold Lake Superior. The hills in the woods are steep, and the trees lift their roots out of the ground in hooks and loops, and make crude staircases up each hill face. I was fifteen years old and very thin during summer camp in the forests away from the Michigan Tech campus. And the days were long for me, and my boots were heavy with mud, collecting ferns and brambles with each step. Pulling each other uphill, bracing each other downhill, we moved in human chains between peaks and valleys. I don't know how the wolves climb the earth there, but we followed them this way for days ....

....
....
....
....*Since I was seven years old, I've had a fascination with wolves. My bedroom was always decked out with wolf models and statues, posters, and collages of National Geographic photos. On my bookshelf were at least ten or twelve books about wolves, their behavior, and their environments. Three of these are by Dr. David Mech, my hero for a number of years*...
....

....
....
....
....The man who led us through the woods was named Ben. Thirty-something with a close-shaved head, he had lost the front four teeth of his upper jaw (from a hockey accident, we figured). And while the rest of us carefully pushed the brush aside and gingerly unwound the vines from our bodies as we climbed, he shattered his way through the branches with a machete, his thick bare arms and neck covered in rows of thin scratches. And while we scanned the horizon for swift, gray movement, Ben would kneel at intervals to read the signatures of phantoms in the snapped twigs and upturned soil of the woods..

....
....
....
....

....*I would spend hours reading the books, sometimes simply looking at the photographs of wolves hunting and research teams tranquilizing and examining the animals. In the backyard, I would pretend our jungle gym was a helicopter and lean over the railing of the slide tower with my squirt gun, select a specimen from the imaginary pack racing across the plains below me, take careful aim, and fire a dart into the left haunch. A perfect hit...*

....
....
....
....

.............................Ben made a living out of finding. Made the actions seem so simple: walk and walk and roll some dirt between fingers or thumb a bruised fern or pinky-test the temperature of a turd on a trail. And from this, supposedly, wolves appeared...

....
....

....
....

......*Wolf crap, or "scat," is particularly telling of a wolf's recent behavior. The temperature, consistency, and shreds of undigested bone and fur create a kind of map. Because wolves use their mouths to interact with the world, bits of where they've been show up in their shit. I read that in one of Dr. Mech's books*..
....

....
....

....
....

....
....

....At the top of a hill, twelve teenagers try to catch their breaths and sip from their canteens to the subtle *beep-ding-beep* of Ben's radio box. He nods, counting the seconds between beeps as he walks around us in a slow circle with the antenna held over his head like a shaman's wand. The gaps between the sounds are getting shorter now, and Ben tells us that a wolf he collared in the spring must be within three miles or so. There's a den over the next ridge, he tells us. Perhaps the wolf is using it...
....

....
....*Dr. Mech talks about wolf dens in* The Wolf: The Ecology and Behavior of an Endangered Species. *Mother wolves try to make dens out of naturally existing shelters. Rocky caves, thickets of vegetation, abandoned fox and badger burrows. Wolves are resourceful animals. They use what the woods provide*..
....

....
....

....
....We cling to
saplings and fallen logs on the other side of the hill as we lower
ourselves into a new valley. A hundred feet down? A hundred and
fifty? Maybe it's best I can't eyeball distance or depth. No one talks,
all concentrating on the placement of their feet. I try to trace the
path of the girl in front of me. Her boots have found decent footing,
good friction despite the mud and dew. Left. Right. A careful
balance, a steady
rhythm...
....

....
....

....
....

....*Dr.*
Mech never really mentioned much about the actual hike to find wolves
in the woods. Maybe I just wasn't paying
attention.................................

....
....
....
....

.....A bird rushes out of a tree overhead. I look up. A mistake. I
trip over a stump and tumble a few paces until I strike a tree
shoulder first. There's a blunt pain beneath flannel on bark. And
I've cut my cheek on a pine bough. Ben looks back, having heard the
noise. He tells the line to keep moving...

....
....
....
....Beyond the clearing, the woods are just as
thick as before and the undergrowth comes up to your knees. How
did he find a den in all this? How does he know he can find it
again?.............................

....
....

....
....

....
..........I am last to reach the top of the ridge. Ben is looking down
into a ravine through his binoculars, pointing to the base of a tree.
It's a hole, just a dark dot in the distance. He presses a finger to his
lips and gestures for us to follow before slinking noiselessly along a
fallen birch. Are we expected not to make noise? Are we to learn
perfect silence in this
moment?...
....

....
....Ben is down the
slope in a matter of minutes, leaving the rest of us to wince at the
pains still in our chests, at the crunch of leaves and twigs we try
desperately to avoid. At the base of the hill, Ben crouches and slows
his steps. With long cat-like strides, he nears the den and stands on
a stump with muscles tensed as if to pounce. His back to us, Ben
raises his machete. We halt...............................

....
....
....
....
....
....................................Quiet...
....

....
....

....
....Twelve
teenagers wait, staring at Ben's still form against the foliage. Some
of the others slowly sink to crouch or lean into the steep slope to
rest their ankles. I lean against an oak to hide my shoulder as I rub
the
bruise...
....

....
....

Steve Dudas

Ben steps down from his stump. He looks back up the hill at his tattered troops, shakes his head, and waves us on with his machete. No signs of activity—bones, scratch marks, fur. No one is using the den...

....

....

....

....

..............By the time we reach him, Ben has a new plan. In another three miles, we'll cross the train tracks and take another reading with the radio...

....

....

....

....

.......Three miles...

....

....

....

....There are frustrated whispers. A girl behind me holds her hand to her mouth to stifle the start of a cry. Is this what we signed up for? Is this what being a biologist will entail? How many scratches and bruises and mosquito bites were edited out of the National Geographic films we fell in love with as little kids? How many hills did *they* have to fumble over, how many hours of walking to get those camera shots? How long can one do this before giving up?...

....

....

....*Dr. Mech has been researching wolves in the wild since 1958.*

....

....

....

....

....The sap on my palms and fingers from clinging to so many trees has collected bits of bark and leaves. My hands are like scaly fishes. I haven't noticed until now. This valley is flatter with few trees. Wading single-file through the long grass, the others examine their wounds and pick burs and bugs from their hair as we walk...

....
....
....
....

....
....
....
....

...............................Ben has not looked back at us for some time. He stares at the untrudged path ahead with his machete hanging from its strap at his belt. His eyes, fixed on the mass of this last hill across this meadow. A balding hill, one thinly peppered with trees...

....
....

....
....

....The world does not exist on either side of him. He does not look for the easy route up the next hill. Perhaps he knows there is none. He will cut or break or smash his way through whatever rises from the ground before him. Obstacles are not obstacles. Forward, always forward...
....

....
....

....
....
....On the new hill, the roots of the trees don't make themselves available to pull ourselves up by. Looking up,

Steve Dudas

Ben tells us that the railroad tracks run across the top. They will lead us back to the river, which we can follow to the van. Ben climbs. He leaps from tree to tree, wrapping his fingers around each trunk and shoving the hill beneath him with a force and speed that twelve hours of hiking should have drained from him.................................

....

....Once more, we follow..................................

....

....Twelve teenagers push themselves uphill. They slip now more than they have all day. They grab each other by the arm and pull one another from tree to tree. Ben is over the ridge before we have reached the halfway point. We crack our muscles against the fatigue and the wounds. We shred our blistered hands on bark. We work this way for nearly an hour..

....

....Near the top, I can see Ben holding the antenna and the radio box. I can hear the nearly gapless *beep-ding-beep*. He does not look at us, but whispers that she's out there. That we are almost on top of her. He sets the equipment down and puts his hands in his pockets.

....

....................................Where?..He does not answer. I creep out onto the train tracks. Gaze into the vastness of the spotless brown sea of waving grass..

....

....
....

....
....
....
....
....
....
....
....
....
....

....
....
....
....
....

....
....
....
....
....
....
....
....
....
....

....
....
....Nothing...........................
....
....
....
....
....
....

....
....
....
....

....
....
....
....
....

....
....
....
....
....
....
....
....
....

....
....
....
....
....

....
....A line of figures
on the railroad tracks. Evening's coming. Or at least the very late
afternoon. And Ben is the only one standing anymore, watching the
wind in the grass. And the rest of us decide amongst ourselves that
the walk back will most likely kill us. This is the last hike, the last
day of camp. Our last chance to see a
wolf..
....

....
....
....
....

....
...........................She's there, Ben says............

....
.......................Hiding. Like a good girl............

....
....The best way to see her, he tells us...........

....
.........Means her secret is safe with us...........

....
....

....
....

....A few jaws hang dumbly open as Ben cracks his back and picks up his gear. He tells us that it is time to go. We have done all we can do. The real job. The way it works..

....
....

..................................Ben leads us down the tracks, taking three ties with each long stride. We trudge behind him, the soles of our boots scraping the wood planks and shuffling the gravel between...........

....
....
....
....On the first morning of camp, we sat around a fire pit between the cabins. Ben went over the rules for hiking through the woods: no running ahead of the group, no dawdling behind, no collecting souvenirs without permission. He told us a few stories about his favorite hikes. Finding pups. Stumbling upon two wolves at a fresh kill. I asked Ben if he knew of Dr. Mech's work, if he had ever met him...
He had...

....
....

....
....

...............................Don't much care for that guy, he told me. A show-off. Kind of an ass.........................

....
....

....
....

....
....
....
....
....*At*
my parents' house, there are three boxes collecting dust in my bedroom
closet. In them, nearly a decade of old wolf stuff. All the models and
statues, the posters and collages I made................................

....
....
....
....
................*One of the boxes is mostly filled with VHS tapes labeled in*
my sloppy handwriting. They're recordings of PBS specials. Wolves of
the North. With the Pack. *Dr. Mech did some of these*
documentaries...
......

....
....

....
....
....*One film ends with a shot of*
him, bundled up with important gear strapped to his body, walking off
into the tundra to find white wolves somewhere in the
snow...
....

....
....
....
....
....
....
....

....
....
....

....

....

....

....

....

....

....

....

.... *I haven't been back to those*

boxes in years ....

....

....

....

....

....

....

....

....

Steve Dudas

Good Housekeeping

Diane Payne

"Are you sure the woman's last name is Brasher?" I ask my caseworker.

"Yep."

"It can't be. They have at least five kids. Why do they need a cleaning girl?"

"Maybe that's why. You should be glad we found work for you."

"I'd rather clean the city parks. Why can't I have one of those jobs?"

"Those are for boys. You clean houses."

Once again, Community Action House called to say they found me a job. Once again it's cleaning houses, only this time it's Paul Brasher's house. This is worse than cleaning the old lady's house. Paul's one grade ahead of me and looks like a model. I never dare speak to him in the hallway at school, but all of us girls talk about him.

"Ma, do I really need to make money?" I ask after returning home from the interview.

"If you want new school clothes, you do."

"But I have to clean Paul Brasher's house."

"Who's he?"

"Only the cutest boy in the entire school. I'll pick blueberries instead."

"Oh, no you don't. All you do out there is flirt with boys and hitchhike to the beach. You need to work."

"But, Ma, how would you like to be scrubbing a boy's toilet?"

"I'd be proud to have a job. You'll develop character. He ain't gonna look down on you. Do a good job cleaning and he may even like you."

"Oh, yeah, boys go crazy over girls pushing mops. Everybody will find out about this."

"Well, I won't tell nobody."

"I know you. Soon as I leave the house, you'll be calling your sisters telling them I got a job cleaning a rich family's house. You'll all be blabbering in Dutch about how much money I'll be making. One dollar and sixty-five cents an hour. That's less than minimum wage."

"You ain't old enough to get those jobs yet. Be glad you got this. All you do is complain."

"I gotta ride my bike all the way out to Lake Macatawa to get to their house."

"You can use the exercise."

"Ma, what do you think I'll be doing out there all day? Watching TV?"

There's nothing left to say. The next day I'm to begin my character-building lessons. I'll never tell my friends about this job. Some of them had even danced with Paul, and they talked about it for weeks afterward. Now I'd be dancing with his mop and telling no one.

Riding my bike past all the fancy houses to the Brashers' house, I wonder what it'd be like to live so close to the beach that you could actually smell the water from your bedroom window. I imagine myself sitting on the patio watching the boats head toward the channel, ready to erupt onto Lake Michigan.

I want to be at the beach. I'd like to walk all the way to Wisconsin, following the shore. Maybe that's not even possible. If there's a will, there's a way. So they say.

But then I come up to the Brashers' street and watch the house numbers instead. All the homes are large. Next to the rest, theirs doesn't stand out. Deep down I was hoping it would have at least been one of the old mansions, but it's just a big house for a large family.

"Good, you're here. What time is it?" Mrs. Brasher greets me at the door. "Five minutes early. I like that. I've fired others, lots of them, just for being late. I've had some stupid girls. Their mothers haven't taught them anything about cleaning houses. Follow me. You can start in this small bathroom. My lazy kids are still sleeping. They think they're too good to clean a bathroom." Then she repeats herself, only much louder this time round. "My lazy kids are upstairs in bed thinking they're too good to clean the house."

I say nothing, just take the toilet bowl cleaner and start on my first task, hoping I'll finish cleaning the house before the kids get up. Mrs. Brasher walks to the kitchen and keeps talking to herself, or so I hope, because I don't know what she's talking about. Since I never respond, she probably thinks I'm stupid, and if I'm lucky she'll fire me.

"This looks good," she says. "I don't care about those damn kids of mine. Turn the vacuum on and do the floors down here. That ought to wake them up. Look at the clock. It's almost eight. Bet your mother doesn't let you sleep in, does she?"

Without answering, I just turn on the vacuum and start pushing it around the living room. There are family portraits plastered on the walls. I look at the pictures of Paul when he was young, all the way until he was fourteen.

One son must be in Vietnam because there's one of him in uniform. I didn't think rich kids had to go to Nam. I wonder how he ended up there.

"Are you getting behind the furniture?" she screams over the loud vacuum.

"You want me to move everything?" I yell back.

"Can't you turn that damn thing off when you speak to me?"

I turn it off and she points out which furniture I am expected to move. "One day we'll give this place a good cleaning."

Their house isn't even that dirty. I wouldn't have wasted my money on a cleaning girl until the house really needed a cleaning. I pick up their fancy knick knacks and dust carefully. Mrs. Brasher slams things in the kitchen cupboards, cursing her children, even though they are still upstairs in bed.

"Those damn kids. We've waited long enough. Go to the room on the right and just start cleaning Jessica's room. She's the youngest and will be the easiest to wake. You tell her to get up. Take this dust mop up there and do their floors. Go on the porch and shake the rugs out."

"You just want me to wake her? She doesn't know me."

"That's what I said to do. She'll figure out who you are."

As I walk up the stairs, she calls me back. "Take these underwear up to the boys."

"Now?" I ask.

"Yes, now. I'm paying you to work now. Just hand these to them. Those lazy boys of mine can at least put their own underwear away." Then she raises her voice again, and yells up the stairs, "Can't you lazy boys at least put your underwear away?"

"You want me to go in their room while they're sleeping?"

"I'm paying you to work. Get up there!"

As I walk up the stairs, she starts screaming again. "You lazy kids better get up! The cleaning girl's on her way!"

Everything is worse than I had expected. Both Paul and his younger brother Peter are awake and looking at me when I hand Peter the underwear, but we say nothing. I quickly leave their room and find Jessica's room. She is just getting up. Without exchanging words, she walks past me and heads downstairs. The boys are still in their room so I dust slowly, dreading facing them again.

"Pull those sheets off her bed," Mrs. Brasher screams.

I hadn't heard her climb the stairs and am startled by her presence. "Put these clean ones on." Then she gets her sons out of bed.

"Don't you know how to make a bed?" she asks. "You need to tuck the corners under. In the army, they made you do it like this. If a quarter didn't bounce, you had to do it all over."

"I never heard of that," I admit.

"Your mother hasn't taught you how to make a bed?"

"Well, not like this."

"Then you don't know how to make a bed."

"She wasn't ever in the army."

"Don't be stupid. I wasn't either!"

"I saw a picture of someone in uniform downstairs," I say, hoping to find out how a rich boy got stuck in Nam.

"No wonder it took you so long to vacuum. Don't be nosy while you're here. One picture is of my husband when he was in World War II. The other one is of my oldest son who's in Vietnam. He'll be coming home this summer to get married. You'll have a lot of cleaning to do then."

I didn't know they let the guys have a leave to get married, and can't wait to ask my neighbors about this. The Greens even enrolled their sons in college to keep them out, but one son still got drafted. Maybe if Terry got married, he'd be able to come back home.

As Paul and Peter go down the stairs and I hear their mother yelling, "It's about time you lazy boys got up! Hurry up and eat breakfast! I'm not waiting all day to feed you. I'm paying that girl to clean your room and you two just stay in your beds!"

I know Paul recognizes me from school. If he's anything like my brother, he expects girls to clean his room, even if they aren't family. I just want to get out of their house, so I pull off the sheets and try to put the clean ones on with the corners tucked.

After cleaning their rooms, I go on the upstairs porch, which has a worthless view since it doesn't face Lake Michigan, and start shaking out the rugs. Paul and two of his friends from our school are shooting baskets. I see them pointing at me, but no one waves. Instead of developing those character-building skills, I'm quickly losing face.

"This isn't how you tuck in those corners!" Mrs. Brasher screams at me while I'm on the porch.

I walk over to the bed and receive another corner-tucking lesson. Why can't she just fire me and put me out of my misery? Then she walks on the patio and yells to Paul's friends, "I have to hire a girl to make Paul's bed. I bet you make your own, don't you, Ryan?"

"Will you stop?" Paul screams back.

I think she wants to humiliate both me and her kids, but I may be the only one feeling humiliated. They are used to her.

Finally, I finish, and she hands me ten dollars. Mrs. Brasher wants me to clean twice a week. I don't make ten bucks in an entire week picking berries, so I tell her I'll return, though I hope my caseworker will find me another job.

Riding my bike home, I watch the houses deteriorate the closer I come to my street. I want to turn around and head to the beach. Take a swim. Enough cleaning for others. I want to cleanse me.

I need to get Mom to the beach. She can't swim, but she could watch the sunset. She could feel the power of the lake. Maybe she'd feel better then. Maybe she'd understand me then.

I don't head to the beach. Mom's waiting for me at home. She'll want to hear how my day went cleaning the house. When I reach our block, neighbors shout out greetings, making me feel human again, restoring my lost character that they don't even know I've lost.

"How was the job?" Mom asks.

"Ten bucks," I say, offering nothing else. She can tell I'm angry and lets it be.

I go upstairs and practice making my bed with the corners tucked.

"What are you doing?"

"Ma, this is how they make them in the army, and this is how Mrs. Brasher wants them made."

"That's nonsense. What's wrong with the way I taught you to make beds?"

"She said you ain't taught me right."

"Oh, those people think they know everything. You tuck it in like that and get hot feet at night, how you gonna free those blankets so you can cool off?"

"If a quarter don't bounce on the bed, it ain't made right."

"Those highfalutin people don't know everything. She think I keep a dirty house?"

"She said I knew how to clean the bathroom."

"She probably thinks I ain't taught you nothing 'bout cleaning."

"It's character-building, Ma. Remember?"

Nothing more is said. The next day I'll ride my bike to the beach and pretend this job doesn't exist. I know cleaning this house will involve more than my character being built. This job makes Mom look at her spotless house with a more critical eye. Won't be long and she'll be asking me to show her how Mrs. Brasher makes the beds.

And one rainy day, Mrs. Brasher will offer to bring me home. Then she'll try to find an excuse to see what our house looks like inside. Maybe she'll ask to use our phone, or say she wants to meet my mother; somehow she'll get inside. And then, my mother will receive her lesson in character-building, a lesson she has been taught too many times before. And Mrs. Brasher can tell her friends that she is not only helping a poor kid by hiring me to clean her house, but she is also teaching me to clean my own mother's house. Mrs. Brasher will believe she's the one performing the community service, the one developing character. But I know by the end of the summer, I'll master those character-building lessons, and my housekeeping days will finally be over. And I can't explain it, but I know those lessons will remain with me for a long time.

For now, I'll go to the beach. It'll be the beach and me. Nothing more. I'll take my sleeping bag and sleep in the dunes, far away from the houses waiting to be cleaned. I'll walk for miles. In the winter, I'll make hot chocolate in a cookstove on the icebergs. The beach defines me, not my job. This is the most important lesson that I've learned.

Diane Payne

Hunting the Whitetail

Michael Mayday

Standing was an exercise. I had to shift my weight from the small seat built into the stand to my heels and then to the balls of my feet before putting a good deal of pressure on my quads, which shook from slowly extending. I turned the left side of my body toward the two bucks off in the distance as I brought myself up. The bucks, grazing in the alfalfa field before me, didn't notice my movement. My bow, which I had placed on a small branch to my left, was already in my hand. Slowly, I pulled an arrow from my quiver and notched it. I watched one buck graze by a rub my father and I had traced out to be roughly twenty to twenty-five yards from my stand—the very distance I've been practicing at. As the buck grazed, he exposed its broadside to me, offering the best shot I'd likely get for the season.

I latched the mechanical release to my string and pulled back, tucking a little plastic marker right beside the corner of my lips. I peered down the doughnut eyesight woven into the string and matched it with the plastic neon-pink marker my father had adjusted for twenty yards. I paused for a moment, thought of where to place the neon-pink marker, then raised it to match the buck's upper shoulder. I thought better of it, though, and raised the marker a little higher so it would rest just atop the buck's spine, hovering over an area where the arrow would hopefully drop to hit the buck in the lungs, making for a clean kill. I remembered to bend at the hips to compensate for standing twenty feet up in the air, on the side of a tree. My breathing was hard and I thought I was shaking and I wasn't sure what to do next; I ran a quick mental checklist of everything I had to do before I squeezed the release, but nothing came up. I stood, silently shaking. The adrenaline caused me to think my legs would give way at any moment. They didn't. I thought the bucks would smell me and bolt at any second, or I'd flinch, or that another doe or buck would materialize underneath me and spook at my scent or that a truck, for some reason, would come tearing across the alfalfa field bearing down on the deer or me. None of it happened. All I did was watch the buck raise his head and set one hoof forward and then another, grazing alongside his pal. He was leaving, I thought. I almost panicked, thinking I missed my opportunity, until I remembered one thing my father had said if I found myself in this very situation: make a noise. I made a curt "hurft!" and the buck jerked his head, scanning my tree line. It was now or never. My finger, already on the trigger, had tightened and tightened and tightened.

Before I knew it the arrow had flown from my string with a quiet "thump" and was hurtling toward the standing deer in the distance. I did not move; the last time I moved after loosing an arrow I injured a doe, likely mortally, and never found it because my movement adjusted the arrow's flight path into the animal's stomach—likely resulting in a very painful death with no benefit for either party. I wouldn't risk that again.

The buck didn't move until the arrow hit him. He bolted a few strides, reared his hind legs like he was supposed to after being shot in the kill-zone, and ran under my stand toward the soybean field behind me. I moved my entire body to follow his movement as a precaution (another lesson learned from a previous hunting experience). The buck ran roughly 100 to 120 yards from where the arrow struck him before pausing at the crest of a hill to look back and scan the tree line a second time. I noted the spot where he stood; it would help when it came time to track him. But then the buck did something I didn't expect: his hind legs slunk and he keeled over, almost comically, where he stood in the tan soybean field. I was in disbelief. I had shot him in the heart. I had never done that before.

A month later and I found myself in nearly the exact same situation: two figures emerging from a nearby marsh walking twenty to twenty-five yards before me in the pre-dawn morning. I stood (again, it was an exercise), notched an arrow, and waited for the sun to shine on the dull grayish brown blobs oozing around in the alfalfa field. It only took a few minutes for the amorphous splotches to solidify into two bucks. One was grazing near the rub.

My heart was thumping. I was nervous—nearly as nervous as the last time—but I knew what to do and how to do it. I raised my bow and placed the neon-pink marker right over the buck's spine. Bend slightly at the hips to compensate for the height. Don't shake. Tighten your finger and keep the pink marker right over the buck's spine. No need to huff—this one was still enough. Tighten the finger a little more. It ought to surprise you.

The buck shuddered, leapt, and reared his legs before he fell to the ground where he had been grazing only moments before. For a brief second I thought I had done it again. But I didn't. Something was wrong; the buck hufted, repeatedly, and desperately pawed at the ground. He wasn't dead, he wasn't even nearly dead.

I got on the two-way radio my father gave me before the hunt.

"Dad, I just shot a buck. He dropped right in front of me."

"Good job," he radioed.

"Dad, he isn't dead. He's just laying there. What do I do?"

"Ah, well, stay in your stand," he said. "I'll head over when I'm done."

Done meant nine in the morning. I checked my watch, realizing I had a two-hour wait. I looked out to watch the buck I shot paw at the ground, pause to rest, then occasionally lift his head to search for his friend long gone, before pawing at the ground again.

I had two more arrows in my quiver and decided that I had to take action. I notched one, placed the neon-pink marker right over the buck, who was spread on the ground now, tugged my finger … and missed. Too high. I notched my last arrow and carefully placed the neon-pink marker right on the deer, aiming for the beast's heart. The arrow loosed, arched, dropped, and fell short. Not knowing what to do next, I sunk back onto the stand's seat, watching the buck as he'd occasionally paw at the ground, huft, and turn his head toward me, scanning the tree line for the final blow.

Maybe it needed to bleed out. I decided to shout, hufft loudly, and make weird ghostly noises and screeches while waiting—anything to scare him and get his heart pumping so he would bleed out faster. That was the problem, right? The buck, however, wasn't impressed, nor did the noises accelerate his death. The noises only caused the buck to raise his head over his shoulder in an effort to peer at me, before lazily dropping his head back on the ground, frustrated. He stopped pawing, which was nice.

I was muttering "Just die already" when I heard the distant rumble of the truck. I was relieved, but not eager to face my father. The large red diesel truck rolled around the edge of the woods and down a hill before bringing its loud engine to a stop by the marsh. The buck had heard it, twisting his head to watch as my father got out. My father took a quick look as he stepped down from the truck, before walking around and reaching into the bed. He fiddled around with something (probably his case), before producing his bow (which I couldn't pull) and casually walking over to the buck to investigate the problem. For some reason he was careful to keep his distance as he circled the dying deer. Occasionally, he'd stop, look at an angle, and consider the possibility as the deer peered back at him, before walking around again. Finally satisfied, my father stopped ten yards in front of the deer and pulled an arrow from his quiver.

The buck raised his head to watch. He didn't paw at the ground, he didn't huff, he did nothing—he only looked on as my father notched and drew back in one smooth motion. Dad was careful: he took his time to aim for the heart. The buck just lay, easily watching the operation. The arrow, though, was too quick: a thin black blur darted from my father's bow and into the deer. Everything about the buck had both stayed the same and changed in an instant—the outline of the beast hardened, giving sharp, unnatural angles like stone before my father notched, drew, and shot a second arrow. The beast flinched at that one. His head wavered, as if he were ill, and, as he lowered his head, the harsh outline, which once seemed so permanent, faded. The tightened lines that defined him—that kept him so strangely alive when he had an arrow jutting out of his body—gave way to a round neck, a plump torso, and graceful legs; all sagged into the land beneath it. And with that it was dead—just another lump in the scenery.

My father retrieved his arrows from the corpse before walking over to my stand. He said I could come down now and I nodded. I quietly looped a small rope through my bow, lowering it to the ground before climbing down myself. I was sullen, though my father didn't seem to notice it. We walked out to field dress the corpse— something I would be taking responsibility for, once Dad peeled the skin and sliced the deer open. After retrieving my two failed attempts at mercy, I took a look at the buck. My arrow hit it about three-fourths of the way down its spine, right before its buttocks. It went high and to the left of where I wanted it to go. We loaded the empty body onto the back of the truck, talking about my apparent success, how excited the dogs would be when they saw the deer, how Dad saw nothing all morning and, finally, how my failed shot was likely inevitable.

"Michael, look: you didn't do anything wrong," he said as we drove off in the truck. I felt horrible. I was mad at myself. I shouldn't have taken the shot. "Hell, it's happened to me, too, more times than I care to count. All you need to do is just practice, buddy." I didn't know if he was telling the truth or just trying to comfort me, but I did feel a bit better thinking that I wasn't the only person to screw up so badly. When we got home he hung the deer in the barn while the dogs sat nearby, eagerly waiting for anything they could snatch up and claim as a prize.

Soon after (perhaps a day or two) I walked out to the barn with my bow in hand. I walked past the hanging torso, squeezed through the barn's rear doors, and made my way to the black Styrofoam slates placed in front of four bales of hay. During the summer we'd take those pockmarked slates and use them as floating cushions out on the pond, but they served a different purpose now. A small cross made from duct tape was placed in the middle of the upper slate— where a small deer's heart would be if it stood there. I paced thirty yards, notched an arrow, pulled back, placed the pink marker an inch high to compensate for drop, and loosed. I missed the small cross—high and to the left.

Michael Mayday

My Trail

Benjamin Goluboff

I've sometimes wished I lived by a river. Even a minor river—the cedar-water Mullica, say, in New Jersey's Pine Barrens—would carry the energy of sources and destinations beyond the local. Life would be larger, I'm sure, with a river's traffic going by. What happened in my life instead is probably the next best thing. For the last twenty-odd years, I've lived a short shot from an extraordinary bike trail. My trail goes north–south along Illinois's Lake Border Upland, a glacial moraine on the west shore of Lake Michigan that runs from Racine County in Wisconsin to Winnetka, Illinois, a white-collar suburb of Chicago. The moraine is a broad discontinuous bluff above the lake, and the trail runs almost its whole length. You're three miles above the Wisconsin line at the trail's north end, and at its south end the trail is absorbed into a network of urban bike lanes as you approach the Chicago grid. Two county forest-preserve districts own and maintain parts of it. Other stretches are managed—patched, mowed, cleaned—by officials and civic groups from the eighteen cities and towns it connects.

From Chicago the trail follows the Union Pacific Railroad right of way for thirty miles to the Great Lakes Naval Training Center, a vast complex on the lake that serves as the intake point for every naval recruit in the country. At the Navy base the trail follows a highway underpass beneath the railroad tracks, turns a few clicks west, and takes up the route of a defunct interurban trolley line for most of the remaining eighteen miles to the Wisconsin border. The Google Earth photographs of my trail were taken in summer so we see it slipping in and out of view beneath the canopy of a narrow patchy ribbon of woods between the tracks and the road. Beyond the Navy base, before canopy returns north of Waukegan, Illinois, the photographs catch the trail's crushed-stone surface as a thin white line coursing through the oblongs of a light industrial zone and then on through residential back lots. On GPS maps my trail looks abstract and conceptual, a cubist intimation of a trail. It tracks across the display as a corridor of green.

A lot of hardcore road bikers use my trail. Guys in full-on spandex Lance-alike biker drag do epic north-shore rides, especially south of North Chicago, Illinois, where the trail is pavement. I cut a less imposing figure. Middle-aged nature nerd, politely bewildered by much of what confronts me out there, I idle along at an easy pace, birding, botanizing, and musing at the parade as it passes me by. The bike trail may be chief among the reasons I will never amount to anything in life. From thaw to frost, the whole bike-able year round, I am forever sneaking out to my trail—to catch the Big Bluestem grass when it turns red in fall, or to see the first spring Trilliums.

One thing about my trail we have to get out of the way early is that sometimes it smells nasty. This is because Abbott Laboratories, the pharmaceutical giant, has facilities in North Chicago, a city of thirty-two thousand people, mainly black and Hispanic. Abbott is sending up a plume of something in North Chicago that smells like the soluble disinfectant cakes they put in urinals. I'm informed that what I smell on the trail—miles from North Chicago on days with north or south winds—is a masking agent that covers an even funkier smell. It's something I've decided I don't wish to look into further because I know what I'll find will be dismaying. And I'm not even sure how I feel about the smell. On hot, still days the Abbott stank can be oppressive and menacing. But some days, as with the many deformities I've come to accept because they are my poor own, it just smells like my particular corner of the woods.

The bike trail crosses an extraordinarily sharp socioeconomic boundary line at the Navy base. The communities to the south are, in general, white, affluent bedroom-and-country-club suburbs.

Think of them as John Cheever's "hill towns" with Midwestern vowels. In the two northernmost towns before Great Lakes—Lake Forest and Lake Bluff—the affluence takes on a very WASPy and Republican cast. Once the summer haven of the big Chicago meatpacking families, the towns now shelter a population of barons and brokers from new money and old. But ride north past the Navy base and into North Chicago proper and it's a whole different thing. In 2007 the median price of a house or condo in Lake Forest was almost ten times greater than in North Chicago; median household income was more than five times greater. In Lake Forest men wear slacks with little whales or cocktail shakers on them. In North Chicago there's a barbecue place where they've posted Obama's words about how brothers ought to pull up their pants. In Lake Forest and Bluff Mexican nannies take the local kids to parks laid out beneath ancient oaks. In North Chicago (the locals affectionately call it No-go) Mexican and black kids use playgrounds set along the old trolley route that carries the bike trail.

One reason why the boundary feels so sharp is that just before the base, at the very north end of Lake Bluff, there is a parcel of land so big and open that it could only be the preserve of the super rich. It's all across the street from the bike trail, along the lakefront. There's a high-end country club so toney that it hides its countenance from the road behind ten acres of mouth-watering oak-hickory woods. South of that is Crab Tree Farm: almost a square mile of native woods, pine plantation, pasture, and remnant prairie. I've been inside the compound a handful of times with the group that does the Audubon spring bird count, but the place remains mysterious to me. Someone's got a little private menagerie of waterfowl installed there at a year-round fountain. Guinea fowl and domestic turkeys sometimes cross the road from Crab Tree and strut along my trail. In the years that I've been riding the trail the great pasture at Crab Tree has been variously a hobby farm, a polo grounds, and the place where the local Episcopalians bless their pets.

It takes the Spandex people who routinely cross this frontier about three minutes to go from the rich people's trail to the poor people's trail. That's how steep the drop is. A lot of Lake Forest and Bluffers turn back at the Navy base; some have told me they didn't know the trail went farther than the base, and asked if I weren't afraid to ride through the, ahem, bad neighborhoods of Waukegan and North Chicago. I am informed that American conversations about what is and is not a bad neighborhood are part of what the cognoscenti call the performance of whiteness. Which leaves me a little bewildered about what I'm performing when I cross the line. The fact is I have never felt afraid anywhere on the trail. Goofy-looking white guy riding a Brand X bike, or stooping to interrogate a plant in the trailside ditch: I figure nobody's paying attention.

Two miles west of the trail in Lake Forest stands one of the last deep-soil oak savannas in the Midwest, which makes it among the last on planet Earth. A mile east of the trail in Kenosha County, Wisconsin, there's a heartbreakingly rare patch of original dune prairie, which is the only place I've ever seen the fringed gentian bloom. And the trail itself has great botanical interest, if you're riding slow and looking down. In the degraded Buckthorn-Box Elder woods that grow by the trail just south of the Navy base there's a little community of Cream gentian (*Gentiana flava*), which shows that before the woods were here this part of the lakeshore was prairie. There's a break in the canopy above the gentians, and through it enough sun has come to stir up relict seeds from a bygone era. *Flava* has a big shouldery profile and snapdragonish flowers in an off-white that makes you think of fashionable upholsteries and wallpapers.

Here and there along my route are little pockets of the Dog violet (*Viola conspersa*), a state-endangered species identifiable by its long-spurred flowers and the structure of its stem. *Conspersa's* presence in a landscape indicates the survival of a high-quality woodland edge habitat. In downtown Waukegan a little unmowable fold in the trail's grassy margin keeps alive a group of Prairie dock (*Silphium terebinthinaceum*), a signature plant of the mesic or tallgrass prairie. Right along the trail just north of a tough little town called Zion, there are three populations of the Nodding Lady's Tresses Orchid (*Spiranthes cernua*): tiny white orchids arrayed in spirals around delicate five-inch stems. What kills me about the Zion orchids is their managing every year to bloom right in the trail's mowed margin. Out of what evolutionary drama their adaptive cunning was born I cannot imagine, but every August when I find them in bloom they are standing in freshly cut grass.

Through North Chicago the trail is gardened. All along the old trolley route the locals have planted truck gardens. Tax Day is considered the last chance of frost in northern Illinois; people with rototillers are out on the trail then, turning up last year's beds or cutting new ones into the grassy shoulder. Aside from the stuff that's garden staples everywhere, the North Chicago gardeners grow southern black specialties: okra, mustard and collard greens, pinto beans, and watermelons.

Once as I was riding south through the gardens of North Chicago, an old black man hailed me from a newly turned bed. Would I help him lift his rototiller up into the bed of his pickup truck? I asked him what he was planting as we hoisted the machine. Crowder peas, he told me, and I thought I was hearing him wrong. Crowder peas, he told me twice more, before I saw that the problem was me. My botany, it seems, is white-guy botany. I can tell Solomon's seal from False Solomon's seal from Starry False Solomon's seal, but I never heard of Crowder peas. The gardens of North Chicago offer potent images: an ancient black woman in a headscarf chopping weeds with a hoe, rows of beans ripening against a fence where taggers have been, August corn tasseling in the tainted air. The Crowder pea incident has taught me to wonder how much I don't see as I ride the gardens.

Where the trail follows a highway underpass to slip under the tracks at the Navy base, someone has planted a dozen young Kentucky Coffee Trees (*Gymnocladus dioicus*), an odd and pleasing choice for the site. Kin to the Locusts, the Coffee Trees are native to the mid-Atlantic states and are used as urban trees in many eastern states. Locally, they've been championed by the mighty Chicago Botanic Garden whose imprint in north shore landscaping is very deep. This is a tree for winter interest: rough slabby bark and an open branching habit give the Coffee tree a blunt and primitive silhouette.

Over the years I've often seen hawks perched in the Coffee trees, especially in spring and fall when the birds are on the move. The western shore of Lake Michigan is part of an ancient migration route for many of the bird species that breed in north-central North

America. The hawks travel during the day and many of the others move at night to avoid them. The best times to look for hawks in my neighborhood are fall days when a cold front combines with west winds. The front brings the birds down to us; the west wind pushes them toward the lake, where they lose the thermal updrafts they need to stay aloft efficiently. On days like this hawks stack up along the lakeshore.

I'm coming to believe that the Navy base portion of the bike trail exerts some kind of powerful raptor mojo. It's a place of long sightlines, and this aids the predators and the watchers both. The base is set back deeply from the tracks and the road. The land around the underpass is broad and open. Along the trail there is no hedgerow and there are no mature trees. It also helps that the roof of the small Great Lakes train station is home to a population of delectable Rock Doves, the common city pigeon.

By train, bike, and car, I've ticked off a fair checklist of Navy base raptor sightings over the years: two peregrine falcons flying toward the lake together, a female and a juvenile, she carrying unidentified prey; Kestrels hunting the railroad right of way; a Merlin, the mid-sized model of the three Eastern falcons, perched in a Coffee tree and drawing a bead on a House sparrow foraging trailside; Cooper's hawks sallying out from the country club woods to try for the train station pigeons.

My Navy base raptors list has been a slow-moving project, but there was one evening when it seemed like all the birds came at once. In September of 2005 I rode home north as an extraordinarily large migratory group of Common Nighthawks was going south. The Nighthawk (*Chordeiles minor*) is a hawk in name only. Like the Whip-poor-will, a member of the Nightjar family, the Nighthawk is an insect-eating bird whose cryptic markings enable it to roost invisibly during the day. Most of its business is done at dawn and dusk. Its summer breeding range extends across all of the United States except the extreme southwest, then north through the breadth of Canada as far as the bottom of Nunavut and the Northwest Territories.

Here at midlife I've seen three true wildlife spectacles: cranes on the Platte River, raptors at Whitefish Point in Lake Superior, and shorebirds at Brigantine, New Jersey. My bike trail nighthawks were not on this scale, but the emotion they provoked belongs in the same ballpark. This is the emotion earlier speakers of English named the sublime, meaning by that term beauty perceived with fear or awe. Hawthorne at Niagara, or Powell on the Colorado experienced the sublime of volume and dimension. The wildlife sublime—Audubon and the Passenger Pigeon, Farley Mowat and the Caribou in their spring passage—is always the sublime of big numbers.

The numbers on the night I'm talking about—the last hour of warm September light, clear ceiling and lots of dragonflies on the move—seemed bottomless. I first became aware of the birds near the south end of Lake Bluff: a dozen birds, twenty, tree-topping in a little grove of oaks north of the train station. As I stopped to watch, their numbers grew and the airspace above the grove became a complex of multiple flight paths. I pushed off into the hedgerow trail above Lake Bluff hoping there'd be more to see when I came out at the open sightlines of the Navy base.

If you crack the bird's camouflage and manage to see a Nighthawk on the ground or in a tree, what you'll see is as an ungainly unbirdlike creature with a wide mouth and a reptilian look. In flight the bird is transformed to a creature of extraordinary grace. Its pointed wings are steeply recurved, each marked at the wrist with a white band that flashes as the bird banks into the sideways light of the declining sun. Adapted to chase insects on the wing, Nighthawks are nimble flyers, adept at sudden turns and at something like a mid-air panic stop. I never get tired of looking at them.

Coming out of the hedgerow below Great Lakes I saw quite a few more birds, and by the time I got to North Chicago it was clear a major migratory passage was under way. Birds were visible out to the vanishing point in every direction. Single birds flying aloof from one another, chasing dragonflies on a hundred different vectors, but all of them trending south: motes in sunbeam, bubbles in soda pop. If there had been two of me standing back to back and watching two horizons, I might have been able to count them all. What I did instead was time their passing: sixteen minutes, me riding slow, before I was behind the last of them. The wildlife sublime always gets me right around the solar plexus; I get the elevator-going-up feeling as the numbers ascend to uncountable. For the past decade Nighthawk populations have been in decline for reasons that range from habitat loss to competition with Ring-billed Gulls. On the night I'm talking about it seemed possible to believe Nighthawks would always be with us.

I wish I could see the trail whole, to see it as God must: instantaneous, complete, its secrets all laid bare in a poised moment with no before and after. The best I can do is to imagine it's a morning in May when the circus has come to Waukegan. They've pitched their tents and parked their animals in the field by the middle school where the trail crosses Washington Street. For a mile up and down, the trail smells of elephant poop. In a buckthorn hedgerow in Lake Bluff a rotting tree stump emerges from an ancient colony of Trout lilies. Tiny pink blossoms are hoist above the lilies' mottled leaves. A true white trillium blooms behind the stump.

Where the trail passes through Zion there's a big white oak where two Cooper's hawks are sharing a limp bloody pouch that used to be a chipmunk. First the smaller he, and then the larger she, has a turn pulling a string of entrails out of the tiny thing. Near the foot of the oak, a crew of little black girls is playing Double Dutch along the trail. They part reluctantly as a biker approaches. Down at Great Lakes, a class of new recruits is jogging down the trail, sweating and panting and savoring the old joke about how Navy stands for Never Again Volunteer Yourself.

In the gardens of North Chicago there's a feral cat moving cautiously through a bed of okra. The tail of a white-footed mouse dangles from the mouth of a coyote as she crosses the trail near the Wisconsin line. At the north end of Waukegan an older gent with a Santa Claus beard pedals south on a recumbent bike; he works in a tool and die shop in the industrial zone near the Navy base. The first spring shoots of Big Bluestem push through last winter's deadfall in a tiny prairie remnant near Crab Tree Farm, and the weird shuttlecock blossoms of a prairie forb called Shooting Star are beginning to deploy.

Black men in work clothes, workers at a North Chicago pallet factory, are lining up for coffee behind a quilted aluminum lunch truck. In a patchy stretch of woods by the trail in Wilmette the

canopy is starting to leaf out. On the woods floor the complex
bloom of the Jack in the Pulpit—spathe and spadix, the botanists
call it—composes itself like an origami masterpiece. Where the trail
passes the high school in Lake Forest a sixteen-year-old boy is
standing screened by the narrow woods along the tracks. He is the
scion of some banker or actuary. He's wearing a Che Guevara
T-shirt, smoking a fatty, and he knows to a moral certainty that he's
the wildest thing on the trail.

The cognoscenti have pretty much settled it by now: wilderness
and wildness are cultural constructions. Like gender, like national
identity, wildness means only what a particular community needs it
to mean at a particular moment in history. This comes as a great
relief to me; I used to sweat things so. I used to worry about
whether the Little Bluestem grass growing on the embankments at
the Great Lakes underpass was planted by enlightened civil
engineers, or was a survival of Illinois's Ur-flora. Then there was the
problem of the fenced swale. Between the trail and the tracks, right
across from the main gates of the Navy base, there's a long wet
gully. The navy put a security fence around it after September 11,
2001, and in spite or because of the fence the swale has become a
magic place for me. Young Cottonwoods grow in the bottom, and a
little higher up there's a stand of Grey dogwood, whose leaves crisp
up red in the fall. A wild plum tree (*Prunus americana*) grows right
up against the wire. Every September, as a stations-of-the-cross
thing, I eat exactly one of its harsh hard fruits. Once, weirdly until I
remembered it was October and the rut was upon him, a six-point
buck stood in the narrow fenced place when I rode by in the
morning, and was gone when I came back that night.

The swale was a problem to me because I felt I had to figure out
how wild it was. Was it an original feature of the Lake Border
Upland's topography, or was it merely an artifact of highway and
railroad building? I rode along my trail trying to assemble a
hierarchy of authentic wildness, as if there were such a thing. Like
the time an honest-to-God Ruffed grouse flew across my path near
the millionaire acres of Crab Tree Farm. By an act of will I tried to
imagine the grouse as a wildling blown from the north woods by a
freak of weather, and not a captive stocked for target practice.
Something like this hierarchy was in play one spring afternoon

when I rode up on a couple of morel mushroom hunters on a woody stretch of trail in Lake Bluff. They were carrying Ziploc bags of the tender crannied fungus and one was boasting about the take into his cell phone. How uncool, how extractive, I thought and rode by feeling greener than thou. Then another spring came and I found myself doing exactly the same thing—not on the trail, but back in the dunes behind Waukegan beach where I'd gone with a friend to see a Tricolored heron that had lost its bearings and been spotted there.

My trail traverses four lakeside zip codes. It is a link—even if they don't use it as such—between rich and poor. Under fragrant billows of industrial waste, beneath the vectors of migrant raptors, it travels through prairie and parking lot, truck garden and country club. It is every bit wild enough for me.

Lake Erie Spring

Michael Andreoni

In the early morning chill the flare of ardor, so phosphorescent a few hours ago, is sputtering, nearly asphyxiated by the burden of a long winter's expectations. "Why am I here, freezing my butt off?" is the question for Kings and Counselors. The morning mug of life-sustaining hot coffee is clutched protectively while middle-aged bones ease from behind the steering wheel out into the frigidity on which the calendar has seen fit to bestow the title of spring.

There is nothing to recommend in the pre-dawn gloom except the shrouds of mist floating over the water's surface, a nasty reminder that the lake, so recently crystalline, is still warmer than the air nipping at tender extremities. A daunting beginning, but we have evolved under harsher conditions than these to forge ahead in the face of a dismal prospect. A quick inspection of the silver-dark surface reveals that the weather service has got it right (for once), as a reassuring absence of breaking waves bears out the forecast of a two-foot chop—at least in-shore. Back to the car now, for the five-minute drive up-river to the marina, where the mistress awaits.

Newly awakened in the promiscuous false spring of prior weeks, she gleams alluringly under the sodium lights. Tugging coquettishly at mooring lines stretched taut against the last of the high-water current, her spring makeover of paint and wax hide the inevitable stress cracks of age. A mercurial lover for all her beauty, she is possessed of an uncanny knack for embarrassingly public breakdowns just when the bank account is at lowest ebb.

All is forgiven, though, this morning, as milady's engine obligingly starts at a touch, the deep, throbbing pulse a promise of renewed affection. Flick on the running lights, cast the lines, and let the eager current point the bow downstream, nosing into the eddies slowly, with a cautious eye for the burden of logs carried on the spring flood. The growing light reveals a river awash in silt and tree trunks, a rich brown effluvium of earth and wood and sex. The spawn is on, and only the water's impenetrable opacity shields the eye from dirty, fishy love consummating a mere fifteen feet under the hull.

Along the bank the heron plays spoil-sport among last year's reeds, snapping up the love struck with cruel equanimity, to dole out lovingly to her brood hidden among the trees. Past the little sand bar, which, if summer ever comes, will be pleased to host the annual egret review, direct from the tropics, strutting through the shallows in full white on white plumage.

Down to the river mouth, to spill into the immensity of this inland sea, to gaze again across the miles of wind patterned wave tops, golden with the new inspiration of sunlight crowning the horizon over Canada. It is springtime on Lake Erie, at last.

There seems to be no lack (regrettably) of helpful individuals who, without ever venturing upon its surface, will marshal the statistics for you on the relative puniness of Lake Erie compared to her siblings. They'll sneeringly point out that she's little more than a boggy depression in the ground next to Huron, Michigan, and Superior, and contains less water than even her more diminutive cousin, Ontario. A long, shallow saucer of a lake, hardly deserving of the title "Great."

Such unhappy people are to be pitied, like the poor fellow who insists on tracing his royal ancestry for you while standing in the check-out line, clutching his coupon for half-priced beans. A few hours excursion upon the lake would do more to affect a new attitude than many days of inebriated argument over average depths, land drainage area, or other criteria bandied about with boozy familiarity by these, the uninitiated.

They would quickly come to share the opinion of many thousands of boaters and fisher folk who love her, who find that a body of water stretching 241 miles, and encompassed by over 800 miles of coastline must be filed under a heading of "large enough for mortals."

Today is not for the instruction of innocents, however, but for renewal, and shaking free of the stale, bunker atmosphere winter imposes as a condition of our survival against the dark months just past. For re-establishing the horizon a comfortable distance beyond the walls we have hunkered down behind, with our books and movies and games, waiting, along with the tulip bulbs, for the sun to come again. Today the lake will show us the meaning of expanded perception as we motor along at a genteel eight knots, drinking in the liquid landscape with the parched desire to once more be part of the order of things; to resume our place among the gulls and cormorants, fish and turtles, as part of the natural fauna of the world.

Gulls wheel and dive around the boat in hopeful expectation of tidbits to be gleaned from a day's fishing, but someone else must provide their lunch today, for the agenda is quite adamantly crammed with nothing at all. A bit of drifting along with the waves, perhaps a new buoy to be investigated and remarked upon, or maybe, after the air warms a bit, a little nap among the surprisingly gentle swells.

Gentle swells are not to be taken for granted, for Lake Erie will punish the unwary. The old girl will rear up and howl in your ear if you're not careful, knock you around until you must run for cover, fervently promising yourself to pay closer attention, next time, to the wind advisories. Boats are tested and found wanting in the closely spaced breaking waves, and hulls that perform flawlessly on placid inland lakes are exposed as mere cockleshells against the pounding of a four-foot chop.

A larger boat is no guarantee of safety or comfort when the gales blow north and east, driving waves of ten-, twelve-, and fourteen-foot heights across the shallow flats of the Western Basin, until even the thousand-foot freighters must nose along cautiously, lest they're blown out of the shipping channels, aground. Bad weather is allowed for, though, and taken in stride by the faithful, a paltry admission price for another season on the big water. Sit on deck and catch up on the latest scuttlebutt with the neighbor in the adjoining slip, who's also waiting for wind-tossed seas to abate.

To be sure, the twenty-first century poses other, more ominous threats to Lake Erie than the occasional spot of dicey weather. Pollution, fish advisories, dead zones, and other risks present a considerable challenge to the preservation of this jewel, which, together with the other Great Lakes, comprises the largest reservoir of easily accessible fresh water on the planet. These problems exist, and must be dealt with effectively if we are serious about our role as caretakers, as avatars of this magnificent lake.

It is worth our best efforts, for Lake Erie is another world, a dreamy, misty dimension where we win reprieve from the tyranny of the daily press of business, the incessant getting of money. Where we might float along, enfolded in something larger than ourselves, to emerge a little different than we were, a little nearer to becoming the people we would like to be. Lake Erie Spring is there for us, for all who believe in her.

Erosion, 1990

Sanford Tweedie

[Love's] uh movin' thing, but still and all, it takes its shape from de
shore it meets, and it's different with every shore.

— Zora Neale Hurston, *Their Eyes Were Watching God*

A growing nor'easter slices across Lake Huron's gray-green
surface. The wind hides behind whitecaps, pushing them along
until, near shore, it rolls the foam tips into curling waves, races past
as they break against shore, and whorls up the hundred-foot cliff. A
gust smacks my mother's small Pontiac as she drives up M-25 just
south of Port Sanilac. She has driven this road countless times and
does nothing except oversteer slightly when the car is broadsided.
At Two-Mile Park, where she and my dad used to go to "neck" as
teenagers, she glances over the bluff, its edge so near because of
years of erosion. Mom cannot see where the water meets land, only
the waves frothing far from shore.

She is on her way to the funeral of Norma, another death in
what has become, of late, a series of waves slamming one after
another onto our family's shores. Norma was my father's aunt, but
as my father is unable to leave the house, Mom represents them
both at the funeral in Sandusky, a small farming community in the
middle of Michigan's thumb. The hour-long drive from my parents'
adopted home of Port Huron to Sandusky follows the shoreline

northward for thirty miles to the small village of Port Sanilac before turning inland. The bluff plays a cat-and-mouse game with the road, sometimes moving far away, other times running right up next to and batting at the asphalt. The pounding waves first eat away at the beach then reach out to the cliff. Water licks at the earth until it deteriorates, bringing the trees, shrubs, and grasses of the embankment down to the lake, where the unremitting water devours them.

My father is undergoing a similar fate. In his late fifties, Dad is now home-bound, the result of myotonic dystrophy, a form of muscular dystrophy that slowly atrophies the muscles, leaving him forever weak, constantly tired, and lacking in coordination. An oxygen line runs to his nostrils, as he is not strong enough to breathe in adequate amounts on his own.

This condition did not just one day proclaim its presence but has been slowly gnawing away at his body and was not diagnosed until Dad was in his late forties. Knowing now how the disease expresses itself, my mother, who grew up two blocks away from my father and started dating him at the beginning of high school, can point to early symptoms: his wavy hair that so attracted her falling out by age nineteen; long, daily naps; a quick smile that drooped over the years. But knowing the diagnosis has not slowed down his body's attrition. Because the walk from bedroom to living room causes him shortness of breath, and the strain on Mom to hold him up as he teeters down the hall has become so difficult, he has finally been forced—for both of their goods—into a wheelchair. Even getting him in and out of the car has become too much for Mom, so he has become anchored to their house.

A few miles up the shore, Mom drives into Port Sanilac, entering the village where the summers of her childhood reside. Her family owned a small cottage across from the lake, where she slept in a cot on the porch, insects plucking at the screen. The conch of the lake pressed to her ear, she fell asleep to the steady kneading of waves on the earth's skin. These waves, forever regenerating themselves, are the lake's only tangible hint of a tenebrous world hidden beneath its glittering surface: silent, delicate dances of fish; plants floating in liquid winds; a fleet of shipwrecks filled with sailors unreleasable and secrets unrevealed. Nights when it stormed—when the wind gusted in from the northeast, shouldering wave after wave against the shore—she lay awake for hours, too aware of her surroundings to sleep. She loved the sound of the pounding surf shattering against the shore, the safety of the room, the crispness of the sheets against skin.

At Port Sanilac's one traffic light—a blinking one at that—Mom turns left, away from the lake. The fifteen-mile ride to Sandusky is without curves. Only an occasional rolling swell alleviates the flatness of farmland. Although the largest town in Michigan's thumb and the county seat, Sandusky remains little more than a collecting center for the surrounding farms. My parents were born there. Dad's father, a doctor, delivered my mother. This is not surprising since Grandpa and his brother, Zed, also a doctor, delivered most of the babies in the area for thirty-five years. I have heard both of my parents reminisce about old flames, and how my sisters and I could have had so-and-so as one of our parents, but I think they talk like this because of how little doubt there ever was that they would end up together. It seems that in rural areas especially the possibility of fate becomes much more feasible since the opportunities are fewer.

As are all the family deaths, Norma's arrangements are handled by Hackers—sounding like a bad joke to the uninitiated, but no more than the last name of the family who runs the funeral home. My mother walks into the familiar surroundings and surveys the room. Except for the body at the front, the color of the casket, and another person missing from those paying their respects, nothing seems changed since the other funerals, so many in recent years: Norma; her husband, Zed, a year and a half before; my mom's own mother two years earlier; my dad's parents prior to that. Even the flowers seem unchanged, as if they have been here alive and vibrant since the funeral home was built.

Arlon Hacker emerges through a door. Somewhere in the midst of the family death parade, he has taken over the funeral home from his father. Arlon is a large man and looks as if he could move a body around with ease. Yet, as he greets my mother, his handshake is soft, his words almost whispered.

Because Norma was almost eighty and spent much of her later years in her native Alabama, Mom is surprised by the number of people who show up for the service. She has forgotten that in a small town it is difficult to push the elderly and the ill into unseen crevices, since there are so few in which to disappear.

Afterward, leaving the draped rooms of the funeral home, the grieving find that the weather has turned. Snow has begun to fall and the wind has picked up. Mom tucks her head, bends into the wind, and heads for her car. Most of the crowd recongregates at Norma and Zed's house where the armchair in which Norma was found dead, a letter opener inserted into a half-opened envelope, remains empty until the Conklin girl, not coincidentally the only person under forty in attendance, drops into it.

Mom keeps sneaking peeks outside to check the weather. Finally, she feels she has stayed long enough to excuse herself without offending. She passes along more condolences, says her goodbyes, and is on her way home to my father to relate what he has missed. As she steps outside though she realizes the view from behind the sheers has deceived her. Snow slaps her face. She hurries to the car but is already cold and disheveled by the time she pulls the door closed.

Mom starts the car and turns on the windshield wipers. They push aside the accumulated snow. Beyond, there is nothing. Whiteness envelops, darkening the car. She gets out and brushes off the other windows, but the car is still dark. She ponders going back inside, but thinks of her own home and decides to attempt it. Mom pulls away from Norma's house, not sure of what awaits her.

She points the car toward Lake Huron and begins to creep out of town into the teeth of a blizzard whose gale-force winds would have, in an earlier era and a different season, sunk many a ship. She tries to follow the road, the straight line from here to the lake, but cannot find it. Snow obliterates man-made markers. Mom hunkers forward a few inches, moving closer to the wheel, as if this will improve her view. Inside the car, she begins to feel claustrophobic, cracks the window. Snow whips through and eddies in the back seat. It is ten minutes before she reaches the one-mile corner. She does some quick calculations in her head, considers the even more treacherous shore road, and guesses where to turn in. She noses the car onto the crossroad. Unable to see behind her, she guesses again and backs up, managing to avoid the ditches. With the car pointed back toward Sandusky, Mom rolls down her window further against the constricting car.

Back at Norma's, she tells everyone how awful the roads are. Those who live nearby stay a few minutes more then leave. Those from out of town decide to spend the night at Sandusky's only motel, a half mile west of town. These include Bonnie, a woman my mother grew up with, and Terry, my dad's younger brother whose myotonic dystrophy echoes Dad's. Though his future is foretold, Terry can still get around with a cane.

Phone calls are made to inform people of their whereabouts, including one to my sister Suzette, who must now go stay with Dad. Finally, the small group gathers in Terry's room for the evening, remembering Norma, mutual friends, the Sandusky of their youth. It is after midnight when Mom returns to her room. The wind has stopped; heavy flakes float to the ground. She opens the door to a room identical to the one she has spent the last several hours in: low dresser, wooden table with matching chairs under the window, two double beds.

At home, Dad sleeps in a room with another pair of beds, one of them an old polio bed. Soon after my father's condition was diagnosed, the huge, motorized contraption was brought in. The bed oscillates up and down like a seesaw, forcing my father's diaphragm to keep him breathing as he sleeps. The engine's low hum is similar to a boat's motor from fifty feet away when your head is under the water. It is Suzette's turn to empty the plastic urinals and convince Dad not to crawl from the bed in the middle of the night after his oxygen line slips out and he becomes disoriented.

In Sandusky, Mom turns off the bedside light and pulls the covers over her. It is silent both inside the room and out. She waits. No sleep. Longer. Nothing. She sighs and pulls herself from the bed. In the darkness, she shuffles toward the bathroom, her hand outstretched before her. Mom feels the wall, moves along it until it opens into a doorway. She reaches around and flips a switch. The fluorescent light above the bathroom mirror flickers to life; my mother blinks in its glare. She flips the other switch. The fan whirs to life. She turns off the first switch again.

Back in the open room, Mom flips on another light and moves to the heater. When she twists the thermostat knob, the blower rattles to life. Light off again, she shuffles back to bed and in the familiar humming noise of night, among the room's pulsations of life and death, Mom falls asleep, imagining my father rocking gently nearby.

Fifteen miles to the east, morning brings a new landscape. The beach has lost ten, twenty-five, even fifty feet in spots. Trees have been uprooted and spit out a mile or more down the shore. Steel jetties have collapsed under the waves. Lake Huron remains, unrelenting in its reclamation. Mom gets in her car and heads toward that shore, toward home.

Michibilly

Griffin Jackson

The bottoms of clouds were lit yellow and geese flew in crooked arrows overhead. Somewhere south it must have been spring. Douglas Lake, however, did not know. The frozen tundra that was Pellston, Michigan, was a snowglobe. I could scarcely recall the warmth of old seasons.

Inhaling the crisp cool air, I followed the flock of geese as they soared north to a place where it was still winter. The place I stood on the edge of the lake was a strand of shore between snow-covered ground and snow-covered ice. And watching the birds, breathing the cool pine air, I walked out onto the snowy plain, because it was open and nice and because, for a city slicker like me, the opportunity presented itself so rarely.

Snow crunching. Packing it down onto ice with every step. I walked until the shadows of the trees couldn't reach me, on open water turned to glass.

I looked up. Looked down. Felt the snow and cool air. I jumped, just to do it. Just to tempt the ice. I probably looked stupid jumping alone, but so what?

And then, breaking my quiet, cool world, I heard her.

"Wanna see my hole?"

The heck, I thought. I would have considered it longer, but I was distracted by the, how can I put this, *intriguing* woman who had said it.

She'd called to me from an ice-fishing shanty thirty yards away. She looked like the stereotypical Michibilly. You know: the Escanaba, wild, smoky type. Not to be judgmental, but she even had the flannel. Her clothes were ratty and didn't fit. Baggy jeans, boots crowned with the fur of an unrecognizable animal. I bet she killed it herself. Her University of Michigan jacket did not fit her ensemble. It was bright yellow, double XL, and looked new except for a hole in the shoulder. I wondered if she'd killed a man and taken his jacket. By the look of her, it didn't seem out of the question.

"Wanna see my hole?" she said again. She must have noticed that I'd frozen, bewildered. Was it obvious that I was a downstate kid? She pointed to the shanty.

"Oh—" I said, stalling. "Um, okay." I didn't want to insult her. I walked toward the flannel that creeped over the maize jacket.

"Mornin'," she said.

"Good morning."

"How ya' doing?"

"I'm good. How are you?"

"Great. Beauty of a day for fishin'."

"Mmhmm, yeah," I said stupidly. "You caught anything?"

A new, low voice came from behind the shanty and said, "Got a pike this mornin'." The owner of the voice stepped out from behind the little shack.

I stopped. He was imposing. Not in the towering, intimidating way, but in the beer-belly, I-might-have-a-handgun-in-my-pocket sort of way. He coughed up chewing tobacco and spit brown mud onto the ice. Seeing me, he stood up as tall as he could, which was not very tall, but his shoulders were huge.

This is not good, I thought. They were nice—very nice. I've heard murderers are nice before they kill you. Hannibal Lecter: nice guy, but then he eats your liver. The fishing poles with three-pronged hooks the size of tridents didn't help.

You idiot, I thought. These are sweet people. Saints, probably. Church-going, country folk who wouldn't hurt a fly except during hunting season. So what if they probably had concealed weapons. It's a free country. This is Pellston. There has never been a murder in Pellston.

Already within a few yards of the shanty, I couldn't get away even if I wanted to. This guy could shoot a deer on the run from a hundred yards. His eyes told me.

I walked up to them. They don't kill people in Pellston, I reminded myself. But then I noticed something like blood on the snow. Small red pools soaked into a slushy mix. There were minnows, brown and dirty, some of them torn, near the red spots.

It couldn't be blood. Couldn't be.

Reaching the clearing on the ice, avoiding the stains, smelling their Marlboros, and seeing how unkempt they really were, my mind stumbled. Images of *Fargo* and *Deliverance* came to mind. Small town, woodsy folks do kill people. They have axes and recurve bows and ice picks and sawed-off shotguns.

This could be bad.

"Wanna see my hole?" she said again.

What could I say? I'd already come this far.

"Sure," I surrendered.

Of course nothing was going to happen, I told myself, unconvinced.

"Right in here." She pointed to the shanty. "Just sit down in there."

I decided I'd stand a better chance in the shanty anyway. They wouldn't be able to come at me at the same time. I walked in, but not before looking at the sky again, just in case.

Sitting down on an icy stool with a torn cushion, I looked over the hole, but couldn't see much. She stood at the door, I in the dark. She was silhouetted in daylight.

"I'll shut the door. Your eyes need to adjust."

I hadn't expected this. I didn't have a chance to say anything. She flung the door shut. I heard her shut the latch from the outside. I'm dead, I thought. They've locked me in. They're going to soak this shanty in gasoline and light it on fire. I heard shuffling on the ice outside. Whispers, rough murmurs seeped under the shanty door. I won't swear that I heard the words "slash" and "clean-up," but I won't swear that I didn't.

Slowly, my eyes did adjust. I looked for exits. The room was smaller than an elevator. There was the latched door and a two-by-three-foot hole through two feet of ice. Two feet of glistening ice. I looked through and my eyes were caught by the world beneath. Through the hole there was a soundless, beautiful place. This other-world, frozen in a state of rest unknown to the world above, may have been miles below the surface; it was so foreign in its peace.

A five-inch decoy hovered perfectly still in the green and yellow glow. It was mesmerizing. I could have looked down into that water for hours, but the hushed, abrupt movements outside jolted me back. I'm dead, I thought again.

The whispering stopped. The latch clicked. This is it.

I clenched my fists. I was pretty sure I could take the woman. She did not look agile. I only had to figure out what to do if the man pulled a gun. I decided I would take my chances trying to push him into the hole.

The door creaked. No time to formulate a better plan.

"Hey, there," she roared. "How's my hole?" Her face was wild with excitement, but she didn't lunge at me.

I didn't say anything at first. The only thing I could think of were her hands, whether they were clenched or reaching into the flannel pockets under her coat.

"What'd ya' think?" she tried again.

"Nice," I muttered.

"I think I'm just gonna join ya' in here for a bit."

I didn't say anything. She pushed her way in, backing me into the corner. It was tight with the two of us. It would have been tight with just her. Before she closed the door, I saw her pull something long and metal in from outside. She had a spear.

This is it. There wasn't a doubt in my mind; this woman is going to harpoon me like a fish in this shanty and there's nothing I can do about it. Where do these people get things like this? Do they sell spears at Walmart? Don't they have background checks? I wouldn't sell a sharp projectile to these people. And I would sell a sharp projectile to almost anyone. The Second Amendment has been abused. Maybe, if I died, Obama would tighten it up so crazy people couldn't have spears.

The man latched the door from the outside. We were trapped together, the woman and I. What was he doing outside? Why had she come in here with me?

At first, only her eyes glowed in the fresh darkness—and the tip of the spear. I couldn't see her. I could only hear her breathe, and the sound of her crinkling blue-and-maize coat as it brushed against the plywood walls. She started talking, but I wasn't listening. I watched the spear. She kept talking about the "hole" and "spearing 'em." Was this woman stable?

Gradually, over seconds, or maybe minutes, my eyes started to work in the dark. Maybe I'd survive.

Eyes on the spear, fists still tight, something sharp and narrow poked me in the torso. I jumped off the stool and slipped on the ice. She flinched. I almost fell in her hole. The cold air mingled with fear had made me numb, so I don't know if I would have felt the pain anyway.

"Sorry, hon," she said. "Just wanted to give you a poke to make sure you were listening."

I thought about swinging.

She pulled her long-nailed finger out of my side.

I wasn't dying.

"Think I'm going to head back," I said.

"You sure?"

"Yeah. I think so."

"Okay," she said.

She knocked and the man opened the door. I jumped out. He was there, smoking, looking rugged. His expression seemed to say that my appearance was unexpected.

"Thanks," was all I could manage.

"Anytime," she said.

He looked at me, then at the spear.

I nodded and started quickly across the ice. I was still numb. The couple murmured something as I left. All I could make out was, "...he got away."

Selected Poems by Anca Vlasopolos

Anca Vlasopolos

On Saint Clair Pier

corralled in the marina
lines sing out against masts
sheep bells at eve

before me
winds drive a shadow across waters already
ultramarine pretending to be seas

the only salt
runs down my cheeks
clouds hang sulfurous
wiping the sun from skies

perhaps
they say
this is the happiest
of life
already like the time of day
crepuscular

this goldfoil gilt
on sails on whitecaps left in the wakes
on gull bellies and upturned acrobat
swallows
swiftly
going
grey

Anca Vlasopolos

Mere Forage

in late spring over the cement slab dropped in the water
whenever the humans built this sea wall
they appeared
so evanescent so slim so small
as if someone had cut a winter's soggy leaf
to shreds
and threw it in the lake

on days of fury they were nowhere
        that is nowhere my eyes could see

in summer heat i stopped my voyeurism
the path to this small public access to the lake
too sunny to be borne

        in starting desolation of fewer-bird september
        today the water gently waved like sheets in breeze
        lit like a photograph made with mercury tints
the school (why do we name such gatherings to mirror our
arrangements?)
was there again
this time
these gizzard shad
        dorosoma the ancients called them for their lance-like
shapes
        centuries later called skipjack for their leaps
now grown to fingerlings
allow me microsecond glimpses of growing bodies
        the tell-tale beauty mark on silver so pale so polished
        no one even in lakeside mansions owns
they stick together still
knowing what i did not
that they
who gladden through seasons eyes tired of lake's emptiness
are mere "forage" if that
for what
we truly prize

56

Lake Secrets

the two days while i could still hear
my soles strike pavement before the turn   i saw

masses of them mid-lake
lifting above water in straggling V's

swan males in full sail like galleons
as if for courting of the coming snows

they read the water much in advance
of our poor weather radars

over three nights the skin of waves
glossed into green-dark ice

lakeshore disturbed only by distant roar of motors
lake now a mirror for our imaginings

somewhere below those depths
a longtime skeleton once looked out of green-dark irises

somewhere trapped beneath
a newer body not yet given to stripping time

one having seen to his taut shrouds
in summer pride of craft

the other engulfed inside her mind
even before that final jetée to crystallizing flows

Anca Vlasopolos

Lake Companions

I

the day you were here and came
with me to the lake
even though we talked and laughed
the water sulked
dull
still
as if sealed in plastic

but as you took photos that will
i know
make the lake
and me
younger
and better-looking

an out-of-nowhere current
moved
under smooth surface
shoved
before it
a mass of water
that
startled
smashed against sea walls
reached
for your lens

II

the day after you left
a brisk nearly
autumnal breeze
wrinkled
a now showy blue-green
expanse
spangled

with late light

lovers on this patch of grass
at the end of the cul-de-sac street
lay
right under the sign
against loitering swimming breathing
here
where
not so hidden
by maimed shrubs of monster house
one of those statuettes
      of a caricatured black
      awaiting
      bestowal
      of hat
      coat
      cane
bows over the driveway

still
these transgressors
are straight
young
and white

the dog and i silent
avert our glances
look   to the white flag of cormorant throat
            doing its disappearing acts
      to graceless plops
          of teen mallards
      breach of huge bass
          maybe aiming to change
      elements

Anca Vlasopolos

overhead
swallows
fly like
a quiver
shot
all at once
thus far
without aim

Elements of the Pasty and Its Relation to the Lake

Matthew Gavin Frank

Originally printed in the Black Warrior Review

It's not like this with cream of mushroom soup and La Choy fried onions. In the pasty, in the singular shell, dinner shares space with dessert. We start with dinner and eat downward. It's not like this with Hot Dish, with casserole, with pizza with a Saltine crust. In the pasty is an eating toward—a sinking into the bottom of food. In this way, eating mimics drowning. Ambiance mimics drowning. In the pasty, is difficulty breathing, is eyes adjusting to the mineshaft dark and to the daylight, is anticipation, is harbinger, is a whole new world beyond the chuck and the rutabaga, is apples-and-cinnamon, is an eating toward, and an eating toward sweetness.

*

It's not like this with backyard swimming pools, the face-down hair fanning the surface, the beach ball rolling pink over green. In Lake Superior, drowning is an expected tragedy. It's dark at the bottom of a lake.

*

According to the Great Lakes Surf Rescue Project (GLSRP), "Overall since 2010, 210 people have drowned in the Great Lakes (74 in 2010; 87 in 2011; and 49 to date in 2012)."

*

"Just unbelievable how these drowning numbers just keep rising week after week," said Dave Benjamin, GLSRP Executive Director of Public Relations. "At this rate we could see well over 100 by the end of the year."

*

After days in mineshaft darkness, my uncle, or somebody's uncle, or so many of our uncles, swear by backstroking in Lake Superior. It has to do with currents, tides, white-caps. It has to do with everything wet and huge and cool enough to float on. If a body of water this large isn't killing us, Uncle says, it's supporting our weight.

*

Like the dessert section of the pasty, the number 100 is something to reach for, to attain. 100 is a milestone. A goal, sweet and morbid. A perfect, even number. Nothing is more even, more steady, than the hands of the drowned. Not even 100.

*

Like the mine, Lake Superior supports its own agriculture. Off the shore of my hometown, in 2010, the body of Rod Nilsestuen, Wisconsin Secretary of Agriculture, was found floating in Lake Superior.

*

My uncle has a bumper sticker that says FUCK CORNWALL, THIS IS MICHIGAN. If my uncle doesn't have this bumper sticker, then he has black lung, and if he doesn't have black lung, then he's depressed due to a lack of light, and if he's not depressed due to a lack of light, he can call this only soul-sickness, can only lament the ways in which we're not jacketed in pastry dough brushed with egg yolk, a crust that will protect us from birds who scream from the dark, from the lack of air that, in the beginning, seemed to exhilarate.

*

ANIMALS DROWN AT LAKE SUPERIOR ZOO, reads the headline, and Uncle laughs. It's his one day off. He's just come back from his swim, for lunch.

*

Elements of the Pasty and Its Relation to the Lake

This is goal-oriented eating. The meat as a means to an end. Macerated plums on Thursday. The brake to a shaking hand. In the bath of the headlamp is the pasty and the hand that holds it. The batteries here are strong. Once we bite through the crust, release the steam, the heat, the wet, something of the ghost and something of the future, things begin to go cold, dry, the batteries here are the only things that are strong. Tomorrow, I want to lie in bed all day. I wish I lived closer to the Lake. I want to lie in bed all day and listen to whitefish court other whitefish. I want to hear people swimming safely. It's good to have a goal.

*

In Michigan's Upper Peninsula, from 1843 through the 1920s, pure native copper just about leaked from the earth, exploded from it, and towns were established and boomed, and folks ate food and drank liquor and men spread their legs and women spread their legs and with food and liquor and spread legs made descendants who can visit these towns in the name of communion and reunion and union and none, and we call these gatherings *heartfelt* and we call these gatherings *historical*, and we use words like *ancestry* and *inheritance* and we stand on the rock piles and bluffs and tailings of Central Mine and Gay and Mandan and Cliff and Delaware and Phoenix and we eat pasties not because we need to, but because they are some sort of souvenir, some kind of shaft that leads, definitively down, toward something like heritage or lake-bed, something makeshift, but geologic and collapsible, and we pretend that these towns are not popularly preceded by the word *ghost*.

*

The old Phoenix church, in 1858, was called St. Mary's. Later, it was disassembled and rebuilt and renamed The Church of the Assumption.

*

We assume there are meanings in names.

*

Superior derives from the Latin *superiorum* or *superus*, meaning: situated above, or upper. Lake Superior has the greatest depth of the Great Lakes, which means something to a miner. It's something to one day descend into. It's a milestone. Lake Superior has the highest elevation of the Great Lakes, though Uncle backfloats upon it. To the drowned, Lake Superior lives up to its name.

*

Here, to float upon is better than to float within. The upper implies the angelic, though implication is often misleading.

*

The Ontonagon Boulder, of the Upper Peninsula's village of Old Victoria, is a 3,708-pound massif of native copper. It can now be found in the Smithsonian Institute's National Museum of Natural History in Washington, DC, where, should a tourist decide not to read the exhibit's plastic three-by-five-inch placard, he or she will wonder about the specialness of this big, ugly rock.

*

Ontonagon, in the Chippewa language, translates as "Lost Bowl." Regarding the pasty, I'm not sure what this should mean. Regarding the Lake, this is convoluted metaphor at best.

*

According to a travel brochure titled *Visit the Upper Peninsula of Michigan's world famous "Copper Country,"* Old Victoria is "a very picturesque ghost town."

*

The atomic weight of copper is 63.55 grams per mole. The atomic weight of iron is 55.85. The atomic weight of sulfur is 32.07. The atomic weight of gold is 196.97. The average pasty—a baked pastry shell, half of which includes a savory dinner of stewed meat and root vegetable, half of which includes dessert—weighs two pounds. The average human lung weighs about fourteen ounces, so much heavier than this underground air, so much lighter than the pasty.

*

Lake Superior is comparatively obese, but not lazy.

*

While many immigrant miners in the Upper Peninsula were from Cornwall, many more were Finnish, Austrian, Croatian, Italian, Canadian, and Swedish. Each group impacted the pasty's regional evolution, with seasoning, with ingredient. Culinary arguments were fierce. Regardless, each version varied little (those who lived near Superior often used lake water in the dough), and each version was easily portable, heavy and hearty, but clutchable in one hand, and each version, in the cold of the deep, could be heated up on a shovel held over the candle flame of the miner's headlamp. The pasties are cooking. The canaries are screaming. Someone coughs. That means they've not yet drowned.

*

The UP pasty, when compared to the Cornish variety, contained larger chucks of vegetable, a higher ratio of vegetable to meat, encased in a thinner crust.

*

The UP pasty as thin-skinned, even in all of this winter, the weather, and the water, closer to the blood.

*

The UP pasty as a little of this, a little of that, as Yiddish, as Fanagolo, as Esperanto, and the language through which we all can communicate up here/down here, as a means to understanding, as overused symbology, as cliché, as Kumbaya, as all things savory sharing space with all things sweet. As reminder. As anchor. As something even a really big lake can't wash away.

*

Often, a homestead requires leaving home, and then never leaving the homestead. A life of two places. For the subsequent generations, it requires never leaving home in the first place. The pasty as perspective, encased in a hard crust. As riding a snowmobile before you can walk. As backfloating over 100 bodies. As your great-grandson doing the same thing. As *I remember when I* . . . .

*

An 1861 proverb proclaimed that the more ingredients one crams into the pasty, the more protection one has from the devil, as the devil may fear that he may end up as just another ingredient for the filling.

*

In Superior National Forest, over two dozen attractions— islands, campgrounds, inland lakes, waterfalls, trails, jumps (the

Devil's Washtub jump, while technically outside the forest's boundaries, claims lives each year as folks attempt to leap from a cliff, over a series of jagged rocks, into Lake Superior)—are named after the devil.

*

On the playgrounds of the turn-of-the-century UP, schoolboys would sing:

Matthew, Mark, Luke and John
Ate a pasty five feet long,
Bit it once, bit it twice,
Oh, my Lord, it's full of mice.

*

The pasty sits fixed in the hands of the miner, poised, poisoned. The Lake unfixes itself, runs from the hands we eat with.

*

Breton may have said, They lowered a humpback into a copper mine to determine the quality of its air. The human lung can hold only six liters of breath, which is nothing compared to Lake Superior. Where are the headlamps when you need them? My uncle took them into the mine. He says, Whales are the canaries of the ocean. He says, the pasty is no kind of savior.

*

Regarding the Quincy Mine Shelter, from the aforementioned brochure, "Hopefully this historic site will be restored." An eating toward. Before we die, we take the elevator up. As with surfacing from the Lake, it takes a few seconds to recognize the sun.

*

The pasty as doubling back on itself, as a confused plot line, as a figure-eight, Möbius strip, infinity, a late bite downward, toward the sweet, the sweet being closest to the hands.

*

In the candle shadow of the pasty and the birds and the shovel, coughing, we can't tell where umbra becomes penumbra becomes antumbra. We can't tell hands from feet. We can't tell if that's a shadow dying, or a man. We can't tell if the body is broken, or celestial. We can't tell that Lake Superior has been called the Earth's youngest major feature—at only ten thousand years old, a side effect of last retreat of the glaciers. We can't tell that the Lake is tantrumming like a little sister, can't tell that *retreat* is sometimes an answer and, to a superior lake, a Big Bang. We can't tell that our uncles, still young, look so old.

*

So, we eat. And, in swimming after eating, test our ability to stave off the drowning. On the beach, the smell of cooking dinner. Of greasy wax paper unwrapping from pastry shells. In them, the sounds of lakes masquerading as oceans. Sometimes, the sun is out. In it, we must come up to the surface of the earth. We must retreat to the shore. It's lighter there.

Matthew Gavin Frank

South Manitou Island

John. E. Oullet

Growing up in Massachusetts, I was an hour's drive from skiing Killington, hiking Mount Washington, and biking the Cape. Leisure was just as convenient. "Leaf peeping" in Vermont, walking Boston, driving the Maine coast. I was a bike ride from those events that led to the birth of our nation: the Lexington Green, Concord Bridge, and the Freedom Trail. But it wasn't until I was in my thirties that I did a single one.

My job brought my wife, my two young children, and me to Michigan. We settled in Waterford, Oakland County. The year was 1987. Back then it was a relatively painless commute to work in Detroit, down either Woodward or Telegraph to the Lodge. And it was new. My job was exciting. It was worth whatever effort. I learned in my travels that the Davison was the country's first highway, that the stretch of Woodward between Six and Seven Mile was the first paved road, and the Highland Park Ford plant where the assembly line was perfected for the Model T lay wasted and forgotten four miles north of downtown.

Vacations really weren't. They were obligatory trips back home to visit family. But something was missing. I was no longer just a son, a grandson, a nephew. I was a father with obligations of my own, and taking my children home to Boston wasn't good enough.

I didn't want them driving past so many things they knew nothing about. I didn't want them unable to recite Longfellow's "By the rude bridge that arched the flood. . . ." I didn't want them unaware of the horrendous witch trials of Salem. I didn't want them unaware of the Transcendentalist movement of Emerson, Alcott, and Thoreau.

I wanted them to know the ocean and the White Mountains; the Charles River and the Berkshires; the magnificent glacier remains and trees that predated the Pilgrims. But as we visited so many of these sights, another realization came to me: this was my home, and these were things I missed. Their past, present, and future lay eight hundred miles west.

By now I had four children, and not that it became an all-encompassing quest, but I was determined that my children would not leave childhood without knowing the legend of Sleeping Bear dunes, seeing at least one of the over one hundred lighthouses, or visiting the mystery spot of St. Ignace. But life as we lived it was inconveniently in the way. The best we could do for years was the Henry Ford Museum, Greenfield Village, the Zoo, and Frankenmuth. We branched out when all were out of Pampers, to Saugatuck, Traverse City, and Harbor Springs. All were memorable but once again, my plan fell short.

The sites we'd seen were postcard destinations. They were standard themes of "What I did on my summer vacation." Seeing a few neighbors or classmates on a given day was not only not unusual, it was expected. I wanted something unique, something without postcards, something that would make its greatest impression on a summer night when they were retelling it to their own children.

I don't fish. I don't hunt. I'm not a photographer or a collector, so I was looking only for what I would call "an experience." I scoured Michigan magazines that touted the Thumb, the inland lakes, the U.P, and each of the Great Lakes. I watched Michigan Out-of-Doors. I spoke with others. I surveyed maps. Then I spotted it, South Manitou Island, the runt of the litter you can't help feeling sorry for. It followed big brothers North Manitou and Beaver Islands up Lake Michigan on its way to the Straits of Mackinac. It looked harmless yet intriguing, a nice beginner trip to see if it beat the view out a car window driving I-75 at eighty miles per hour.

I broached the trip with my fourteen-year old son, and nine-year-old daughter. I expected a resounding "Yeah, Dad!" from him, and a "You crazy?" from her. Quite the opposite. He was less impressed at the suggestion of an overnight stay.

"I thought you said there were no hotels on the island?" he said.

"I did."

"Oh. I get it," he said dourly.

South Manitou is a three-by-three mile hunk of limestone and cozy, yet fragile, sand dunes carved by the glacier movement of ten thousand years ago. The movement scraped out the whole of the Great Lakes the way a relentless dentist digs through a cavity. Though once a part of Manitou County formed by the kingdom of Beaver Island, it is no longer even worthy of consideration in the Beaver Island archipelago.

The kingdom of Beaver Island appears to have been the heyday for South Manitou, but Manitou County is no more. It was unceremoniously stripped of its charter in 1895 after nearly forty years of lawlessness and disrepute that rivaled Tombstone, Arizona. Without going too far afield from the topic of South Manitou (although out-of-mind and out-of-the-way is consistent with its history), a digression to the rise and fall of Beaver Island kingdom is worth taking.

The Mormon link chart universally follows the line of Joseph Smith to Brigham Young to Salt Lake City, Utah. Few trace Joseph Smith to James J. Strang to Beaver Island, Michigan. Called the Strangites, they arrived on the island in 1848.

Strang founded the town, St. James, established the island's main road {King's Highway), and published northern Michigan's first newspaper. He was twice elected to the state House of Representatives and made the new Manitou County a powerful political force. Then he went and married five women and had himself crowned king, literally, of the church.

The island had non-Strangites, as well, who didn't take a reigning king in stride, especially one who was forcing himself outside his church boundaries. Requisite violence ensued, resulting in islanders plotting against Strang. On June 16, 1856, the U.S. naval gunboat USS Michigan entered the harbor at St. James and invited Strang aboard. As Strang walked down the dock, two men shot him in the back, killing him. The men boarded the ship, which disembarked them on Mackinac Island without arresting them. No one was ever convicted of the murder. The Strangites still exist, some five hundred strong, in Voree, Wisconsin. Another story for another time.

I borrowed two external frame backpacks for the trip. We decided on a three-day, two-night stay. I carried my daughter's things and most of the food. Typical boy, my son would have fit all his supplies in his pockets if he had his way. "I got all I need," he said. It was early August, and hot. "You pack the canteen I bought?" I asked.

"Yeah."

"Is it filled?"

"We're gonna be on an island in a freshwater lake," he said with a shrug. "I can fill up."

"Ah-huh, sunscreen?"

"Long-sleeved shirt."

"Socks, underwear?"

"You're sounding like mom."

"You'll sweat and chafe. Your feet get wet, you'll get blisters and possibly trench foot. And blue jeans? You're wearing blue jeans?"

"You said there was thorns and poison ivy."

As if blue jeans were the only known defenses. I re-inventoried his pack and made adjustments. I allowed the jeans. Suffice to say, the effect of wet denim was a long-lasting lesson for him.

Claimed by Glen Arbor Township of Leelanau County, the island is part of the Sleeping Bear Dunes National Lakeshore. It marks the resting place of the smallest cub who, according to the legend, was unable to make the crossing of Lake Michigan; its mother who now lies in mourning on the mainland dunes (North Manitou being the bigger brother). All the drama of the Strangites seemed to have escaped it. As a matter of fact, everything seemed to bypass South Manitou save the fifty or so ships that sank around the two cubs.

The ferry leaves from Leland. The trip up M-22 along Grand Traverse Bay would have been the worth the time and effort. Sutton's Bay, we all agreed, was just the coolest little place we had ever stopped to take a bathroom break.

Leland is due west. Even crossing over Lake Leelanau was impressive for a boy growing up in New England where New Hampshire's Lake Winnipesaukee was as great as it got. It covers seventy square miles. The smallest Great Lake, Lake Erie, covers nearly ten thousand. Although the Great Lakes were a staple of our geography classes back in the day, the scope of them didn't impress me until I realized Massachusetts is just slightly larger than Lake Erie.

Wikipedia's list of Michigan lakes dwarfs even that of Minnesota, the Land of 10,000 Lakes. Other Internet sites of interesting-but-hardly-reliable information say Michigan has more lakes than any other state in the lower forty-eight with over eleven thousand. Other sites have Wisconsin, Florida, and of course, Minnesota. Either way, it's not even a close second to Alaska's three million. No debate, though, that Michigan has a larger freshwater coastline than any other state or country in the world. That should illicit intriguing thoughts for anyone with an entrepreneurial mind with an environmentalist bent.

We were early for the ferry, so we grabbed breakfast at The Early Bird, a block from the parking lot at Fishtown dock. Good food and convenient. The ride to the island cost seventy-five dollars round-trip for the three of us. Then I plop ten bucks cash for the two nights lodging. Already I was feeling this trip was worth it in so many ways. The Manitou Island Transit, aka the ferry, was three-quarters full, which, frankly, was more crowded than I expected. I wondered how many of them had thrown the proverbial dart as I had, or if maybe there really was something special about the place.

When I told my two we were heading up to an island, they thought Mackinac and a downtown hotel (they knew they were at least a decade away from a stay at Grand Hotel). I sent them to MapQuest with the only hint that it was north of Muskegon. They came back with Drummond, Bois Blanc, Isle Royale, Beaver, Fox, and others I had never considered or even heard of. I was proud

73

South Manitou didn't make the list, as if we were venturing to uncharted land.

They scurried back to the computer when I told them, coming back stunned and confused. "What's there?" they asked.

"Beats me," I shrugged.

It takes ninety minutes to cover the sixteen miles. Grueling for my daughter, who curled into a ball in the middle of the deck, stomach rolling with the tide.

"Picked a day," the captain said as he walked by us. "Never usually this rough."

We landed at the southern tip of the crescent bay. We walked the dock under what was already a broiling sun. They have a four-and-a-half-hour tour, but we didn't need no stinkin' tour. "Where is the furthest camp ground?" I asked the greeting park ranger. He pointed north.

"Popple," he said. Eyeing my littlest, he added, "And hang your food high so you don't attract those northern miniature tigers.

"Chipmunk," he said mercifully before we got out of earshot.

Only three or four groups of us appeared to be making a night of it. They and the day trippers headed south, to where I supposed the other campgrounds were and the tours began. We trekked northward on the main two-track road, leaving civilization behind. It wasn't five minutes before the only sound was the gravel beneath our feet.

The road was lined with scrub bushes and extensive growth of dense pine. It was a simple surprise to see a small schoolhouse along the road. I learned a lesson about doing a modicum of research before setting out on a trip such as this. When my kids asked about it, I hadn't a clue. It wasn't until the next day when we saw the park ranger that we learned about the small, independent farming community that thrived on the island. George Hutzler, a maritime sailor, took a liking to the island as a refuge for his family from the busy streets of Chicago in 1856. Others followed, clear cutting white spruce for growing rye, beans, and peas, which they sold amongst themselves and to the passing ships.

During the mid eighteen-hundreds, the peak years of the waterway that ran the three hundred miles from Chicago through the Straits of Mackinac, a thousand ships a day were said to pass by. The reason was clear enough for even the novice traveler. The half-moon cove on its east side was a natural harbor, offering a degree of safety during the legendary gale winds and storms that were known to erupt out of nowhere. The three days we were there, we counted only five ships, though I'm sure we missed as many.

We arrived at Popple Campground at close to three o'clock. I was excited to see we were the only ones there. It added to the adventure. Remote was the word. There are seven sites but finding them mixed within the scrub bushes was like finding Waldo. My daughter found the stake. Number 6. It was stabbed into the ground around scrub pine and what I was sure was poison ivy, of which there is much. I don't know poison ivy from English Ivy, never have, so any plant that resembled a vine was to be avoided. My son, a boy scout, seemed surer than I that site three was clean so we set up there.

The bluffs overlooking Lake Michigan and North Manitou were inspirational. We sat along them for a while. My wife, less sadistic than I, packed a pair of shorts for my son, which he eagerly put on as soon as we made camp. Taking off his jeans was like a painter stripping varnish. It was good comic relief after the hour-long road march.

After fifteen minutes on the sand, the water beckoned. No sooner did we step off the crest when we were swarmed by black flies. And they bit madly as if famished or very angry for something we might have done. We walked the beach, then ran, in hopes we'd leave them behind. But two hundred yards down they were still with us, or we were handed over to another colony. The water worked but as soon as we got out, the flies came in again for food and beverage. It was unbearable.

We scurried back up the dunes where there was no underestimating the majesty of our perch. We walked the bluffs east and west until nightfall, swatting flies and wiping sweat. "There's nothing here," my daughter said. I wasn't sure she considered that a good thing.

The campsite was thorny and though I trusted my son's training, I scratched in spite of it. The bugs at the campsite were numerous but not so savage, nothing a healthy spread of Off didn't handle. No wonder we were alone, I thought, but I locked on a tight smile. Like my kids I was not gleefully anticipating another day and night at the site. As fate would have it, a wandering couple came by. A man and a woman, mid-thirties, looking very much how real hikers should. We flagged them down as if they were the first civilization we'd seen in months.

They were regular visitors to the Great Lakes' Islands. "We spent a week on the north island in April," they told us. "Cold and wet. But lots of plover activity."

The piping plover, we learned, was an endangered species of bird. There are believed to be no more than twenty-five breeding pairs in existence, a few on North Manitou. (As of this writing, a nesting plover has been spotted on South Manitou.) The hikers knew the region as well as I wished to some day. At least one week each season they spent on one island or another, except Mackinac, which they viewed as no different than the mainland.

"There are deer and beaver over there. Bald eagles."

"How come there are none over here?" my daughter asked no one in particular.

"Not much animal or human life here," the woman said. "You couldn't have picked a more secluded place on a more secluded island." Noticing the dismal look looming over my kids, she said quickly, "You know you can climb the lighthouse on the other end of the island."

"And there's a shipwreck just off shore," the man added. "And the oldest grove of cedars on earth."

"And," the woman added, "no black flies."

After our Sterno-cooked Chef Boyardee dinner, we slipped inside our tent to read and talk, the three of us with visions of a renewed outlook on tomorrow. It must have been how the pioneers felt, knowing they had just one more peak of the Rockies to pass over.

We spent the most enjoyable day and night at the Bay Campground near the dock and a fly-free beach. There was a water supply (none at Popple), and a fire pit (forbidden in the north end). We read beneath tall pines, traversed the fallen cedar that dated back before Columbus, climbed the 117 steps of the lighthouse tower, and stared out at the wreck of the Francisco Morazan. Yes, it was a postcard day.

The family has since canoed the Au Sable River and the Platte. We've done the inner trails of Mackinac. We've kayaked local lakes. We never did do Isle Royale or Pictured Rocks or the big trip, a through-hike of the Appalachian Trail. But in that microcosm of South Manitou Island, we learned a bit about vastness. Scaled down to more manageable parts, one could walk either direction to other experiences. South Manitou gave us a night of solitude and a night of society in a mere three and a half miles.

Our night at the Popple Campground was surely one to forget for a period of time. Now I find it a time for reflection. My son is an Army officer at Fort Bragg, North Carolina. My daughter is away at college. He spends off days on his motorcycle climbing remote roads in the western part of the state. She has traveled to Tanzania and the Serengeti, climbed Mount Greylock, Grandfather Mountain, and Mount Washington. Without trying, I think back on how I watched them break brush and cut their path.

John. E. Oullet

No Dominion

M.J. Iuppa

Living close to Lake Ontario, snow begets more snow. Daylight burns white glare. The air's silver foil hurts teeth. No one smiles much. Everyone leans a shoulder forward—heads bent down, pulling weight-like pack horses—steam slipping from frozen nostrils. Darkness comes early. Sea blue shadows whisper across fields and country roads, carrying cold to doorsteps. Cold wants in—latches onto wool coats and heavy boots. Cold wants us—even by the wood stove, it waits—waits until we crawl into bed, shivering.

This morning in the crabapple tree, a band of robins. Thirty peckish brothers call back and forth—not a summons of *sweet-sweet-low*, but acerbic shouts to be quick. What brandy ferments in fruits' caramel skins? Is it enough to save them? Spoilers—they scissor cut, branch to branch, knocking back a few in large gulps—stirring the tree until it's picked clean.

Everywhere—tracks in new snow—the calligraphy of hoof, paw, claw—all converge to stand still. Is this the treaty they've agreed upon? And when snow melts, what then?

Pinpoints of light on snow gleam briefly. The distance of stars and death has taught us to see what isn't there. *Sleep, wake, sleep, wake.* We wait our turn.

M.J. Iuppa

An Unfamiliar Shoreline

Aram Mrjoian

I had never experienced Lake Michigan from this coast. The Chicago skyline loomed over the beach, an industrial behemoth casting a tall shadow, each building looking out over the coalescence of navy and teal, contrasted against the azure backdrop of the sky. The masts of sailboats poked out of the water like gangly, ashen stumps of birch trees in an infinite blue abyss. Perhaps this was the Midwest's Coney Island, for a vast menagerie of people occupied the shore, basking up the summer sun with indefatigable gusto, well weary of the coming winter, a season they knew would inevitably be harsh and unforgiving. This summer flux of heat seemed in sync with the natural rhythm of these monumental waters, four seasons as distinguishable and unyielding as walls that box together a room, perpendicular in such a way that the people became specular, mirroring each change with natural swiftness from years of adaptation. The crowd en masse conveyed an aura of sun-evoked elation, donning minimal habiliments and roaming about aimlessly in the sand, playing volleyball or tossing a Frisbee, jogging and biking on the cracking cement path, reading, sunbathing, drinking, eating, erecting muddy obelisks and drizzling water across their apogees, or burying one another in the warm skin of earth. The prosaic nature of this scene became personally significant based solely on the overwhelming number of people, the banality evaporating in the heat, evolving into portentous condensation

81

amongst the crowd. This was a moment in time that was by every definition normal, an ordinary occurrence simultaneously experienced by many, and yet, I had never seen so many people on one stretch of beach, and I had never seen this side of the lake before.

Katy lay next to me on her towel, enormous sunglasses covering the majority of her face, dozing in the heat. I wanted to touch her but I was mystified and afraid. We had agreed, though I with protest, to a cessation of physical intimacy, and now she was something natural and ravishing that had been sealed off from me and had to be enjoyed from afar. She suddenly seemed as foreign as the shore, her back a distant, enigmatic expanse, barely concealed beneath a swimsuit, a body I had known thoroughly, now covered up forever, as sharp and dramatic as the change in seasons, my ephemeral summer ending into a timeless ice age. Moreover, while I could do no more than ogle her distantly, I was aware that she was nearly entirely exposed to a tremendous amount of strangers. The pedestrians surrounding us had gained some gifted access to her corporeal attractiveness, and in her idle state she was as remarkable as the lake itself. The landscape in front of me took second place. I was jealous of every person sharing this view with me. How had I ever imagined I could possess this empyrean woman? My fingertips surged with the spectral reflex to glide my hands across her skin. The force in my hands throbbed and almost pulsed.

This was the reality of geographical separation and the cease of physical partnership. I felt the deep pangs of abandonment, but I had been preparing for this moment. Downfall had been imminent for some time. Acmes could only be followed by nadirs, and mimicking Icarus I had felt heat unbearable and now I sat with my skin itchy and singed. All else aside, ideally, there was still a friendship there.

I was nauseous from under eating, drinking too much coffee, and exposing myself to the sun. I felt hollowed and nervous, but the only thing that seemed right to do was sit and focus on breathing. I knew later I would drink alcohol despite not being able to keep it down. My stomach always announced my mood. I had been vomiting all week, terrified of this penultimate closure, knowing the last steps toward ending this relationship forever were hopping on a train, drinking warm Heinekens in solemnness, and returning home to Michigan. What had once seemed a congealed, lifelong camaraderie had fissured and dissipated into disconnectedness and gloom.

My brother had once lost a kite on this same lake in Frankfort, Michigan. We watched it glide off over the water, pushed by a herculean zephyr toward the lake's center, disappearing in the distance, slowly shrinking until it dissipated into nothingness, and when I was younger I always imagined it flying forever southward, eventually reaching this shore. I imagined the multicolored nylon sheet coasting for days, blown by a phantom deity, sending the kite skyward every time it flagged and dove. Could I dig it up amongst these sands? Could anything so unpredictable and uncontrollable be salvaged? When I was younger I had never known what the shore would look like, I could only imagine it, and now I was there, feeling unfamiliar and isolated. It is amazing that a crowd can bring about powerful feelings of loneliness. Only amongst others can one see their genuine individuality, not in a sense of esotericism, but more so as a lone being. While the beach for most was a whimsical, seasonal pleasure I could only momentarily see it as a clamorous barrier between Katy and myself. In reality, the barrier was entirely internal. Outside of her and me no one felt the divide, and summer continued unobstructed.

When I refocused and stared out at the water all things seemed alien. The water was a different hue than from the other side, the sand grittier, the aroma ostensibly urban, harshly juxtaposed to the fishy, fetid odors of its opposite coast, the people seemed hyperbolic and calloused, the traffic behind them obstreperously blaring klaxons of impatience, the noise complemented by the hum of motors and wafts of diaphanous gasoline, the people piling over one another, milling about searching for acquaintances and water fountains, and the woman next to me far away and unreachable, mirroring this shoreline for the first time, reflecting every infinitesimal nuance of this new location, becoming anew entirely, changed into an entity I could not please or satisfy, gorgeous and untouchable, sand clinging to her in aesthetic bliss, her features bronzed and magnetizing, sleeping and unaware of my heavy breathing, toes buried in the beach, her body facing the earth, clinging to her newfound home, morphed into an unknown composition, and for a moment, I longed to be the kite, soaring over the water, headed home.

Memories and Perceptions

Mel Visser

During the past seven decades, I have had the pleasure of hiking Lake Michigan's steamy dunes; canoeing Lake Superior's Pictured Rocks, Keweenaw shores, and Isle Royale; commercial fishing Keweenaw Bay and tasting its November gales; sport fishing Lake Erie's walleye after it "returned from the dead;" sailing Lake Superior's length and breadth; and scuba diving around Isle Royale. I have also had the privilege of a Great Lakes education, thirty-six years of employment in the chemical industry that developed from the basin's resources, and the opportunity to do in-depth study of the Great Lakes lingering and serious chemical contamination by PCBs and banned pesticides.

I have witnessed dramatic changes in the Great Lakes, but the physical changes pale in comparison with the pendulum swings of change in public perception of our lakes. In my youth, the lakes were permanent bastions of creation, immune to the presence of man. As we recovered from years of war and rationing to claim the good life we deserved, rivers feeding the Great Lakes provided convenient waste-removal systems. Somehow, it was difficult for us to identify the environmental destruction caused by uncontrolled agriculture, industry, and municipalities as unwise and unnecessary. By the time cartoonist Walt Kelly had Pogo tell the nation that "We had met the enemy and he is us" (1971), we were leading the effort to restore our lakes and the wildlife dependent upon them.

Mel Visser

One of our most amazing accomplishments was banning of a "Dirty Dozen" persistent organic pollutants (POPs) that had entered commerce after World War II. Great Lakes activists and political leaders were at the forefront of this effort, a feat that historians will someday count as a crowning example of democracy in action. Unfortunately, decades after POPs banning, PCBs remain at sixteen times the International Joint Commission's "fishable" limit in the lower lakes and toxaphene's presence in the "edible flesh" of Lake Superior's lake trout exceeds the level that defines dirt as hazardous waste. The source of this toxicity is currently ignored and toxaphene has been dropped from fish consumption advisories. Public perception of our lakes is once again as far from reality as when we thought they were too robust to be affected by man. I'd like to share my memories of living, working, and recreating in the Great Lakes to focus on the continuing and devastating presence of these "banned" substances.

My first memory of Lake Michigan was an adventure from the Grand Rapids home I was born in to the pier at Saugatuck. Such trips were rare because we were in the midst of World War II and tight gasoline rationing. Michigan's industrial might was uncoupled from the automobile and sent to war. My father, a tool and die maker, was involved in war supplies as mundane as ammunition boxes for Grumman Skyrockets and as exotic as the diamond tooled anti-tank projectiles that knocked Rommel out of the African desert. My father carpooled to save his gasoline ration for regular hunting and fishing trips to supplement our meat ration.

On summer weekends we typically visited nearby lakes where fifty cents rented a boat to troll and cast for pike and bass. I got to row my father and older brother around until I was old enough to handle a bait-casting rig and hand my younger brother the oars. With good planning, my father could fill the 1940 Ford's tank for a "Big Lake" adventure about three times a summer. The Saugatuck trip was special. We'd strap long cane poles to the 1940 Ford, drive to Saugatuck, take a hand-cranked ferry across the Kalamazoo River, and hike over the dune to the pier and the awaiting perch.

Michigan was a gritty state at that time. Every town had smoke-belching power plants and industrial smokestacks. Homes and businesses were heated with furnaces fueled by soot and acid-generating soft coal. Backyard snow was soon covered with sooty black strings and ash. The best use of the Kalamazoo River was perceived as a waste conduit for municipalities and the paper industry. If the Kalamazoo River stank a bit, I would not have noticed it. Compared to whipping the Nips and Krauts, a little stinky water and a few floating fish was a small problem. Besides, a tiny ribbon of water carrying a little pollution could never harm the Big Lake.

In my formative early teens, television came to Grand Rapids, if you had an antenna high enough to reach across Lake Michigan and pick up Milwaukee. The wonders of "Industry on Parade" and advertisements for "Better Things for Better Living through Chemistry" fostered a yearning for chemical engineering. My first exposure to chemicals, although I did not perceive it that way at the time, came as a sixteen-year-old working a summer job in a furniture factory. Metal castings that would end up supporting auditorium seats came down an assembly line like an endless wobbling column of wooden soldiers. I would take them off the line, dip them in a tub of paint, and place them back on the line. Ventilation was minimal, and the solvent for the paint was a mixture of benzene, toluene, and xylene. Benzene was not carcinogenic at that time and by the end of a shift I was wobbly drunk on my feet.

The first environmentalist I met was Doc Bazuin, my Grand Rapids Union High School chemistry teacher, a block away from the Grand River. In the mid 1950s the Grand River basin was not as heavily industrialized as the Kalamazoo, but by today's standards, the Grand was highly polluted. I remember Doc lamenting that, "The Grand River used to have a sizeable trout run and now a self-respecting carp would not be caught dead in it." "We've got to do better," was his plea. I hope he now knows that the Grand supports an exciting salmon run.

I went north to Houghton for my chemical engineering education at the Michigan College of Mining and Technology, now Michigan Technological University. Here, I fell in love with Lake Superior, and a cheerleader from Suomi College, now Finlandia University. Gloria's mother baked pasties the size of a shoebox and her uncles fished a forty-five-foot oak gill-net tug. I married the family and received a great education on Lake Superior as I studied chemical engineering. In my sophomore year at Tech, Sputnik launched and professors informed us of our choice: study hard and catch up, or learn to speak Russian. The only environmental engineers of the time were civil engineers who designed municipal waste treatment plants; chemicals had not yet entered the environment, or so we perceived. Our faith in nature was deep and we knew that flowing water purified itself every hundred yards and earth purified any substance spilled onto it.

From today's viewpoint, the late 1950s environmental perspective of people from Michigan's Copper Country was amusing. A mile or so before Houghton, there was a large, handsomely crafted wooden billboard stating "Welcome to Michigan's Copper Country-You are now breathing the purest, freshest, most vitalizing air on Earth," and they passionately believed that. Just before Houghton, the Ripley smelter came into view across the narrows of Portage Lake. A six-foot diameter stack jutting from the smelter's roof blasted a flame that turned into a reddish yellow plume of oxides of nitrogen to lift soot and particles high into the sky. In town the power company's boiler sent a dense black plume skyward from its lakeshore location. Down the road to Lake Linden, stamp mills crushed ore from mines in the hills into copper chunks and sand. The sand was dumped into Torch Lake, an arm of Portage Lake. Lake Linden's powerhouses, mills, and chemical plants blackened the skies. All municipal and industrial waste went into Torch Lake, untreated. Yet, the perception was that the air and water of the Copper Country was the world's most pure. The trees cleansed the air and Lake Superior was far too large and too cold to ever be polluted by man.

We welcomed PCBs, poly chlorinated biphenyls, as a substitute for flammable mineral oil used to cool electrical equipment. I have several childhood memories of flaming transformers at the top of "telephone" poles and the resulting power outages. PCBs eliminated costly and deadly fires across the nation. This wonder product was tested in other uses and soon worked its way into paint, caulk, plastic, hydraulic fluid, and lubricant applications. One of its most creative uses was an ink carrier that solved a major office problem.

Offices of the 1950s were run by well-dressed women called secretaries who cheerfully brewed coffee for their bosses and made "carbon copies" by placing sheets of black "carbon paper" between sheets of plain paper loaded into their manual typewriters. The Royal or Underwood key would strike the machine's carbon ribbon to transfer "ink" to the original and the force of the key would transfer carbon from the carbon paper to the "carbon copies" layered between sheets of carbon paper underneath. The first carbon copy was legible, the second nearly readable, and the third hardly worth the effort. The carbon paper was messy to fingers, sometimes covered in white dress gloves, and clothing. A wonderful product called no carbon required (NCR), paper was developed and immediately accepted. NCR paper contained ink in a liquid carrier encapsulated in gelatin. A striking typewriter key would break the microcapsules to release ink only where it was needed. No more messy carbon, but a serious unintended consequence resulted.

During the war, paper-recycling plants had grown up along the Fox River in Wisconsin and the Kalamazoo in Michigan. The liquid "carrying" the ink was a PCB mixture. NCR paper contained 3.8 percent by weight of PCBs and through years of ignorance paper recyclers legally discharged hundreds of thousands of pounds of PCBs into river sediments.

We were very familiar with dichlorodiphenyltrichloroethane (DDT) and loved it. A use I appreciated was the Department of Natural Resources' fogging of state parks to rid them of pesky mosquitoes. DDT was known as the "chemical that won the war." In World War I, more soldiers were lost to typhus than to gunshot. Dusting soldiers and prisoners with DDT avoided typhus, and spraying DDT into swamps around bases and battlefields killed malaria-infecting mosquitoes. DDT came home from the war to eradicate malaria in the United States and then went to India and Africa to save millions from malaria. The post-WWII chemical boom gave us a whole new class of persistent organic pesticides such as DDT, toxaphene, chlordane, Lindane, Mirex, Eldrin, and Dieldrin. These chemicals were welcomed as replacements for eternally persistent heavy metal pesticides containing lead, arsenic, and mercury. They did their job and "disappeared" within weeks.

Mel Visser

In the early 1960s parts of Asia and the Middle East were headed for mass starvation. Our humanitarian response was to export western agricultural technology to dramatically increase crop yields. This "Green Revolution" saved hundreds of millions of lives. Through the use of superior seeds, irrigation, fertilizers, and persistent organic pesticides, once-starving countries supported an expanded population and now export food.

In 1959, with a fresh degree in hand, Gloria and I moved to Kalamazoo where I took a job with The Upjohn Company, now Pfizer. We passed up an opportunity to work for Standard Oil of New Jersey, now British Petroleum, as on the interview trip Gloria's eyes burned and she found breathing difficult. She was spoiled by the Copper Country's "pure" air and could not adjust to this land where highway toll takers wore gas masks. While manufacturing penicillin for the war effort, Upjohn developed superior fermentation technology. They had also discovered chemical routes from soy sterols, a byproduct of the soybean industry, to cortisone, hydrocortisone, Medrol, prednisone, prednisolone, and a constant stream of new products. From Kalamazoo, Upjohn supplied the bulk ingredients for a quarter of the world's antibiotics and half of the world's corticosteroids. I was assigned to a process development group with chemists and engineers drawn from all over the world. It was a paradise of creative chemical opportunity.

Upjohn, a family-owned company at the time, was founded by a medical doctor and had developed a corporate culture that believed in taking care of its employees, the community, and the environment. As Upjohn grew, disposal of large amounts of waste antibiotic fermentation beer was becoming a problem. The local paper companies were recognizing the need to stop discharging chalky streams of clay and fiber and the city was still the largest in the nation without a secondary wastewater treatment plant. The Kalamazoo River was dead and weed-choked for miles. Upjohn worked with the city and the paper companies to design and install a tertiary water treatment plant, one of the nation's finest. At that time, nobody recognized PCBs as a problem.

Safely tucked away in a community of scientists making miracle drugs from soybean processing residues and antibiotics from various agricultural processing wastes, I was isolated from the rapidly changing public attitude toward chemicals. Industrial solvents and dry cleaning fluids were showing up in drinking water, and Rachel Carson's *Silent Spring* was questioning environmental degradation as a necessary price of progress. Lake Erie was dead and a river flowing into it caught on fire. Eagles, cormorants, and gulls were disappearing. Our unconditional love affair with chemicals was ending.

Through a rapid and dramatically transformed public perception, industry went from a benevolent supplier of better things for better living to a greedy spoiler of human health and the environment. They, along with municipalities not treating wastes and farmers using poisons to control pests, needed to be controlled. The Clean Water Act, Clean Air Act, and legislation controlling chemical exposure and waste disposal were passed, and rules promulgated and enforced through the newly created Environmental Protection Agency and the Occupational Safety and Health Act. Chemical exposure was correlated with the growing incidence of cancer, and chemicals found to be, or suspected to be, carcinogenic in the laboratory were seriously controlled or banned. Common solvents such as carbon tetrachloride, a cleaning agent present in every household, and benzene, a component of gasoline, were banned. At that time, my perception of these bans was that overdosing petri dishes and laboratory rats could ban any chemical as government officials tried to achieve a ban per week. I was reacting to burden of work placed on us, and a belief that our operating in good conscience was protective of health and the environment. Time has changed that perception.

In a few short years, the public's radical transformation in perception of chemicals and pollution caused many changes in my professional life. My employer, once perceived as a generous and civically active corporate citizen that did well by doing good on all fronts, was now a greed-driven major polluter. With the advent of part-per-billion analytical procedures, our groundwater became contaminated and our air emissions of solvents extreme. We were subjected to an overwhelming array of regulatory requirements. I was transferred from the challenging area of understanding nature's rules to improve chemical processing to the chaos of understanding man's rules and complying with them in a manner that allowed us to stay in business.

In order to comply with federal laws, Michigan's Department of Natural Resources had to work through the legislature to pass laws as protective, or more protective, than the federal law, promulgate rules under these laws, and then enforce the rules. Public hearings were required at many steps of this process. These hearings typically degenerated into catfights between environmental activists, who demanded much more stringent standards to ensure protection of the Great Lakes, and industry, which fought to not be put at a disadvantage to competitors in other parts of the country. I had little sympathy for the DNR at that time, but in looking back they were in a terrible position. They had major projects forced upon them without a commensurate increase in funding or staff, and were getting flack from all sides.

The director of the DNR took a creative approach to address the catfights. He invited (read, forced) a group of industry leaders and the heads of environmental groups together for a few days in the woods. He patiently and clearly showed them that he had a job to do, and he could perform it with improved outcome for industry and the environmentalists if they could seek some common ground instead of disrupting his federally mandated process. These leaders were impressed with the meeting, felt it was very worthwhile to break bread with the enemy, and wanted to create an ongoing industry/environmentalist interaction. A few months later a U.S./Canada group of industry and environmental leaders, the Great Lakes Corporate Environmental Council (GLRCEC), was formed, and I received the honor of being its industrial cochair.

This GLRCEC group worked through their differences and found considerable commonality at their core levels. Through it, I learned much about the presence and effect of chemicals in the Great Lakes environment. At this time, the early 1980s, DDT and PCBs were banned and the United States was well on the way to banning the "dirty dozen." DDT, with its unique ability to thin bird eggs, had nearly eliminated eagles and cormorants, and seriously reduced gull and tern populations. PCBs, toxaphene, chlordane, and dioxins were present in fish in levels that required the development and publishing of fish consumption advisories.

Staying in regular contact with Gloria's commercial fishermen uncles helped me realize the drastic changes in the Great Lakes. Lake Superior, the greatest of lakes, was running out of fish. Lake trout had stopped reproducing in Lake Michigan, and production was diminished in Lake Superior. Trout, herring, and chubs were all depleted. Sea lamprey made a contribution to this devastation, but most of Lake Superior's issues were chemical. I remember Uncle Reino staring out of his gill-net tug, wondering where the windrows of flies went. Were pesticides killing them on the farms and they were no longer getting to the lake as fish food? More likely, if we understood the real source and demise of the flies, they were no longer developing in the POPs toxic lake.

The Erkkila brothers' fishing business continued to decline and was lost entirely as the Indians reclaimed their harvest rights, and the Michigan DNR decided to manage the Great Lakes as sport fisheries. There were no fish left for a business that had been successful for seventy years. The Erkkilas' tug, the majestic "Twin Disc," now fishes out of Bayfield, Wisconsin.

The International Joint Commission (IJC), a U.S./Canada agency charged with oversight of border issues, became very concerned about Great Lakes water quality and in 1975 adopted a Water Quality Agreement that included addressing PCBs and persistent organic pesticides. Their perception was that all contamination was coming from within the Great Lakes Basin and that if sources within the basin could be controlled, the legacy persistent organic pollutants (POPs) would disappear and the lakes would become "fishable." The IJC instituted policies of "virtual elimination" of POPs within the basin and "zero discharge" of POPs. Special binational programs were set up to protect Lake Superior. Immediately after their banning, POP levels fell rapidly, but then leveled off. The only POP that did not decline on banning was toxaphene in Lake Superior. Its concentration increased 25 percent after it was banned. Paper pulp bleaching plants were suspected to be supplying Lake Superior's toxaphene, but intensive studies proved there were no local sources. It was coming from the air, but from where?

By 1991, toxicologists studying POPs were developing serious concerns. In assessing POPs toxicity for banning and fish consumption advice, scientists focused on cancer. With limited data and uncertainty, toxicologists used precautionary factors of safety and we hoped that more data would show POPs to be less toxic. Unfortunately, new data showed POPs to be acting as endocrine disruptors and immune system suppressors at much lower levels than the cancer concern concentrations. Activists renewed their demand for POPs elimination with renewed intensity... and a creative idea.

All POPs contained chlorine. Environmentalists eagerly accepted an idea that continuing use of chlorine in the basin was causing the POPs levels to remain constant. Their theory was that when chlorine and organic material got together there was no predicting what chemicals were formed, so PCBs, toxaphene, Mirex, Aldrin, Dieldrin, chlordane, and the rest of the dirty dozen banned chemicals would be accidently produced as long as chlorine was used. Therefore, banning chlorine from the basin would clear out the banned legacy POPs. This theory had no basis in science or logic, but the perception that greedy local industry had to be the source, and frustration with the recalcitrant toxics was so strong that it was real to the activists. After two years of study it failed to be accepted by the EPA and Environment Canada, as it should have.

During 1994–1995, there was an extensive effort to measure all PCB flows in and out of Lake Michigan to understand the relative magnitude of various sources and plan for their elimination. This "Mass Balance" study showed that the PCB flows from the air to the lake in the winter, and from the lake to the air in the summer, were much larger than inputs from rivers or outputs to sediments. There was a net loss of a thousand kilograms per year to the air. In another study, the PCB content of open ocean air was assessed through long-term measurement of air above Bermuda. This air contained seventy-five million molecules of PCBs per liter and its concentration remained quite constant long after PCBs were banned. The only significant trend noted in this study was that the levels were slightly higher when the wind blew from Africa. From these studies, it certainly appeared that global air and all our northern waters interacted, that the early rapid loss of PCBs from Lake Michigan was to the air, and that global air would limit the loss of PCBs as equilibrium was established. Unfortunately, the EPA and

Environment Canada have ignored global air and remained focused on "environmental recycling" as the reason for constant POP levels.

While the IJC, EPA, and Environment Canada remained focused on the Great Lakes Basin as the POPs ecosystem, international researchers addressed a perplexing arctic contamination problem. Marine mammal fats were found to contain POPs at levels that would classify them as hazardous waste. Chlordane and toxaphene, pesticides never used in the Arctic, supplied 90 percent of the toxicity. International scientists determined that POPs moved through the air and their ecosystem was the northern hemisphere. POPs emissions anywhere in the ecosystem, and pesticide application is a 100 percent emission, would travel through the air, circle the globe, and equilibrate with waters according to their volatility. Lindane races to the Arctic Ocean where it is found at forty times the concentration as oceans in the south. PCBs deposit at mid latitudes and diminish to the north. *Lake Michigan has come into global equilibrium at twice the PCB level as Lake Superior.* Toxaphene loves high mountain lakes and cold, clear waters. *Because of toxaphene, Lake Superior lake trout are North America's most POPs-toxic fish.*

The arctic findings launched global POPs banning efforts that culminated with the Stockholm Convention of 2001. Chlordane, toxaphene, and PCBs were the cause of arctic toxicity, but somehow the ignored these POPs and focused on eliminating DDT and dioxin. UNEP-funded scientists now run computerized models that assume zero POPs enter the ecosystem to "advise policy managers" on the status of POPs. They find that there is no reduction in global concentrations of PCBs, chlordane, and toxaphene, and conclude that POPs continue to recycle in the environment and do not degrade. POPs did not stop degrading; it is our courage to face inconvenient truths that has degraded. Does it matter?

Legacy POPs raining on places remote from current uses are slowly being recognized as a significant global health problem. Blood levels, or known excessive POPs ingestion, correlate with a suite of diseases from cancers to obesity, dementia, intelligence of offspring, infant death, and attention deficit disorders. Research findings, such as the examples below, are often accidental as the belief that chlordane, toxaphene, and PCBs are globally banned is commonly accepted in the medical and science communities.

A few years ago, doctors in Vancouver were surprised to find the blood of non-Hodgkin's lymphoma patients containing three times the chlordane as that of a control group. They were not overly alarmed because chlordane was banned. Nearby, researchers studied the accumulation of emerging POPs in two brown bear populations. One group had access to the salmon run and the other lived off the land. Quite accidentally, they found the salmon-eating bear to be loaded with chlordane and the bear without access to salmon having little to none. Researchers expressed concern about the effect of chlordane on the bears' heath. Meanwhile, line-caught wild salmon's healthy attributes are highly advertised to humans.

We have not been successful in ridding the Great Lakes of POPs by banning them. Continuing to dredge sediments and ream landfills to deposit them in another backyard while global uses still exist will not solve the problem. This local action may be satisfying, but it is like replacing carpeting before fixing the hole in the roof.

It took courage to stand up to our own political, industrial, and agricultural leaders to insist upon the banning of carcinogens. Two generations ago, pride in our Great Lakes led us to lead that effort. Now, the chemicals are still here, they are known to be more toxic, and we know they are coming from foreign sources. Finishing the job started by the Stockholm Convention to ban, or severely restrict PCBs and the legacy POP pesticides, is the only way to make our Great Lakes "fishable." It will be a difficult task as we have been hiding the problem in hopes that it would go away and focused on "thinking globally and acting locally" while the world is creating issues that can only be solved through global action. Hopefully our current generation can understand the global nature of the source of this pollution, realize its global effect on wildlife and human health, and use their passion and skills to create change. Our lakes and our health are too precious to ignore.

The Lake Is a Lady

Robert M. Weir

Originally printed in Michigan OutofDoors

I was a student at Western Michigan University when I first saw her, a turquoise pearl, a vast liquid altar stretching from a threshold of golden sand and wispy green dune grass to a distant sky that covered her like a baby blue blanket. I had ascended the dune from the brushy, inland side with five college friends until we broke from under a canopy of shade and mosquitoes into the daylight of mid May. With the advantage of a two-hundred-feet elevation, I gazed out, down, and upon Lake Michigan. Her beauty held me breathless, and, suddenly, I was unaware of the pretty coed, my date on that clear summer morning, who stood at my side.

Lady Michigan's cool, clean body lay before me. Her gentle waves softly whispered a hushed invitation to race down the dune and plunge into her, to immerse and be absorbed. I swooned at her splendor, hesitated to drink in more of the love-at-first-sight vista, then moved with quickening strides that pounded my soles against slippery sand.

My movement was contagious, my friends' response instantaneous. With coolers, towels, and Frisbees in hand, we descended the dune faster and faster as though we were mere slivers of steel drawn toward a powerful magnet.

We dropped our stuff on the last gentle slope of beach, held hands six abreast, and raced to the edge of the water where two-inch waves lapped the shore. We ran as best as possible until, like children, we were knee-deep and tripped into submersion. We were, I was, part of her, part of the Great Lake that stretches three hundred miles north from Chicago to Mackinac, eighty miles west from Holland to Milwaukee, and is bordered by Illinois, Indiana, Wisconsin, and both peninsulas of Michigan.

Since that day, twenty-seven years ago, I've moved to other parts of the country and back again. I've frolicked in the majestic lady's waves, climbed her dunes, walked her beaches, and sailed along her Michigan shore. I've flirted with her sisters: cold howling Superior, plain wide Huron, shallow Erie, and industrious Ontario; but there is none like Lady Michigan.

Finally, I'm fulfilling my longtime desire to sail across her. There are four of us on two boats. Norm Guillaume and Dan Erlandson on Norm's twenty-six-foot Pearson, Agape, and Dave Davies and me on Dave's thirty-foot C & C, Mega.

Our plan is to go north for two days, from Holland to either Muskegon or White Lake, then head west to a destination in Wisconsin to be determined by the lady's mood and the direction of her winds.

We cruise out of Holland at 8:00 p.m. on Friday, July 21. Winds are light and southerly, the water is sun-drenched and warm, so Norm and Dave drop drag lines, and we take turns being pulled through refreshing seventy-degree-Fahrenheit water.

As we air-dry, Lady Michigan displays her hospitality by presenting a crimson sun formed into a perfect orb, which reflects orange on her green surface and turns house windows on the shore into fiery jack-o'-lantern faces.

At night, she serves brightening stars and stronger southerly winds. The houses become spots of electric white.

Dave and I discuss philosophies of life and unimportant land burdens as we relish the pure, pleasant gurgle of the hull slipping through soothing waters, leaving a small liquid eddy around the tiller that quickly collapses and fills as we continue north.

We're three miles off shore. The lake is 100 feet deep. I'm at the tiller and, ignoring the compass, I set the tip of the port spreader in the middle of the Big Dipper and run parallel to the coast until, near 2:00 a.m., we turn into the channel at Grand Haven, twenty miles from Holland. There, we raft with fifty other boats tied to the wall outside a full municipal marina.

We stroll the summer harbor town in the wee of morn and scope out Dee Lite, the noted eatery where we plan to have breakfast. I sleep on Mega's cockpit bench until awakened by the no-wake passage of the early-morning fishing fleet.

We set sail at nine o'clock on Saturday morning, and strong following winds propel us rapidly. We cruise past the Muskegon pierheads, twelve miles north of Grand Haven, at noon. White Lake, another twelve miles north, seems like a good destination, but we blow by that port in midafternoon, making a commitment to sail around Little Point Sable, which bulges Michigan's curving shoreline westward, until we get to Pentwater, sixty navigation miles north of Grand Haven.

The lady treats us with gentle blue swells most of the day, but when a storm hits in early evening, she changes color as though it were eye shadow, and heavy rain bounces like liquid crystals on deep green rolling concrete and pounds her surf into small submissive waves that gently cradle rock our boats.

We pass Sunday at the marina in Pentwater Lake watching sunfishes race around buoys and other transients pull up to the gas dock. We read, relax, and restock. Bill Smith replaces Dan as crew on Agape, and I think about the upcoming night sailing across Lake Michigan.

For many people, this trip would be no big deal, by no means a Columbus or a Leif Ericson adventure, nothing for the history books. Thousands of mariners plow the Great Lakes toiling on ore and oil freighters. Sailors compete in the famous Chicago-to-Mackinac races that traverse the south/north corridor. Pleasure cruisers in Loran- or GPS-equipped sloops and ketches sail east and west between Michigan and Wisconsin throughout the summer. Go-fast-make-noise power boaters plane from shore to shore in three hours, guaranteed. Even reckless, radioless jet skiers cross the narrower, fifty-mile northern section of the lake between Betsie

Point and Door County. Others have traveled greater oceanic distances, some in unsafe rafts or record-setting miniature boats much smaller than Agape and Mega.

To mariners and pleasure boaters, Lake Michigan is a workplace and a playground, but there are also many Great Lakes natives who sit on the shore without dipping their toes in the water, who have never ventured from the tall dunes, who have never seen the bright lights of shore slip into the distance until only the lake is visible in all directions.

I remind myself of how many years have passed since I first fell in love with this beautiful body of water, how much time before having this opportunity. Too many and too long, resound respective replies. And finally, I'm doing it. For me, this is special.

We leave Pentwater on Sunday at 4:00 p.m. Over the dunes, inland thunderheads billow and furl like uncurried lamb's wool, gently floating away from us. We set a course of 270 degrees, due west. At 6:30, we're eight miles offshore and Michigan, the state, is clearly visible beyond Little Point Sable to the south and Big Sable Point to the north. Not until twenty miles out does the lady hide her terrestrial namesake from view, and then, it's questionable if land disappeared because of the crest in the horizon or the dimming of daylight.

Lady Michigan is kind. She whispers soft southern breezes in our ear, and we glide through the water on a broad reach at a fairly constant four knots until, with a host of stars and the hazy Milky Way overhead, she becomes tired and becalms us. Reluctantly, we resort to piston wind.

Around midnight, she presents a mystery, a lake freighter that appears as a single light to our port in the far southern horizon. Judging from land visibility at dusk, the freighter is, perhaps, twenty miles away when we first see her. For half an hour, we watch her approach, her lights growing brighter and more distinct, until they loom near in the blackness. "We're on a collision course," Dave and I echo.

What's her cargo? I ask myself. Grain from Iowa or Illinois? Or is she empty, having left Pennsylvania coal in the windy city. What's she weigh? Ten thousand tons? Or more? The immensity of the numbers is insignificant. The freighter is huge and fast, depth perception is deceptive on the water at night, and I'm anxious to steer clear.

Dave attempts radio contact with Norm and Bill, who are a couple hundred yards ahead of us. They're not concerned and hold their westerly course. I turn the tiller and head Mega south to allow the freighter to pass to our starboard.

Dave talks to someone in the freighter's pilothouse. The big ship responds with both voice communication and a beam bright enough to spotlight a demasted sailboard at five miles. It blinds our eyes, but I'm relieved to know she sees us. The voice in the pilothouse tells us to turn our course west and pass. We do and the big freighter begins to fade into the distance.

Dave and I are confused. The ship appeared on our port, and now she's steaming away to our starboard even though we didn't seem to cross either her bow or her stern. I hope that conversation with Bill and Norm the next day, along with spoons positioned and maneuvered on a restaurant table, will clarify the confusion, but without our friends' perspective and the aid of dining utensils, the mystery floats, unresolved, in my mind and, like the freighter's blending stern lights, becomes less and less clear. We again make radio contact with Bill and Norm, and their chiding offers no solutions, so we laugh and shrug it off as one of the unraveled seafaring mysteries of night.

With the hint of dawn, the lady is as gentle and vibrant as she is mysterious. She kisses our eyelids with early morning dew, and as though serving breakfast in bed along with stimulating conversation, she offers a bright predawn cloud the shape and color of a fiery forked dragon's tongue. She tops this with a rising, thin, crescent-shaped fairy tale moon.

Then she suddenly turns a cold shoulder and, with dense fog, secrets Wisconsin from our view until we nearly stumble into the Port Washington pierhead at high noon, twenty mostly sleepless hours after leaving her eastern shore. The harbor, a mere three hundred yards inland, is clear and sunny, reminding us the lady has a personality that defies her land neighbors.

We sleep Monday afternoon, visit with friends in the evening, and stroll the town before Norm and Dave take five guests out for a late-night motor cruise on Mega.

On Tuesday, Bill buys a wooden hand-carved sea gull with a three-foot wingspan that raises a controversy of whether he or the bird will sleep in his berth. We joke that, if Norm lashes it to the bow pulpit, it'll provide extra lift and speed.

Lady Michigan is placid as we start our return trip. Leaving at noon, we motor south along the shore until encountering an area where bearpaw ripples border channels of flat calm. We shut off the motor at 2:00 p.m., turn east, and steer toward the burred, nail-file surface in search of wind. A few miles off shore, the lady presents perfect southwesterly breezes. She wears blue, and we frolic, sometimes dipsy-doodling the two boats a half mile apart and sometimes running so close that Dave, standing on Mega's bow, passes peanut-butter-and-jelly sandwiches to Norm, holding onto Agape's transom lifeline. They celebrate the moment with high fives while Bill and I hold course.

As day becomes evening, the lady dons a black gown capped with fringes of white froth. Over her Wisconsin shoulders, she throws a black rain veil highlighted with white and pink lightning.

We continue to run with full sail, watching the distant storm slowly gain on us. Winds increase as night and the storm close in, silhouetting Agape, to our stern, in bright celestial flashes. The lady begins to rock 'n' roll, and Dave and I replace a 150 genoa with a self-tacking working jib. Dave says, "The time to reef the main is when you first think about it," and we follow his instincts.

When crossing to Wisconsin, the lake confused us. On this return trip, she's confused. Waves can't decide whether to precede the storm coming from the southwest or to respond to clocking winds that now blow strong out of the north.

I go forward and take down the jib as Dave holds the tiller as steady as possible in seas that follow from both the starboard rear quarter and the port rear quarter. I attempt to put a second reef in the main, but when I release the halyard, the howling wind holds it tight and unmovable against the starboard spreader and stays.

When lightning threatens above us, Lady Michigan seems to change her mind about the storm. The winds die, and our speed drops from eight-plus knots to less than two. We take advantage of the lull, and I drop the main as Dave starts the engine. He tells me he's heard stories of storm gusts tearing out webbed bungie cords like the one that holds our roughly folded sail to the boom, so I take two spare dock lines and make sure the main is securely tethered.

We're twenty-two miles out and mercury vapor lights from Muskegon glow, dead ahead, on the horizon. Grand Haven is a dimmer luminescence to the south. Dave says, "It's time to get off the lake," and we motor in the last three hours while the lady chops at us with two-fisted rogues.

I'm disappointed that we had to start the motor, but I acquiesce to Dave's wisdom, and we part the pierheads of Muskegon at 1:00 a.m., eleven hours after turning east, slightly more than half the time of our westerly crossing.

We're dry as we tie up in transient slips at Harbor Towne. We've outrun the storm, and I've accomplished something I've wanted to do for many years. I've shared two wonderful sleepless nights in the watery bosom of Lady Michigan.

Robert M. Weir

Generational Power of the Big Lake

Donald M. Hassler

Geography shapes our lives and often guides what we write. Chaucer made that road trip to Canterbury. Washington Irving wrote New York and, even Columbus, as both idea and city. Jerusalem and its environs generated competing faiths. My older son is now the principal investigator for the radiation experiment with the *Curiosity* rover on Mars, intended literally to see if we can settle there. Usually, my own writing lives in the cool country of the activist folk singer like Tom Paxton or Greg Brown, who used to make his northern tour every summer around the Keweenaw, where my wife and I have our summer camp. But Paxton grew up in rural Oklahoma, and my wife dated him in Norman when they both were college students there. So getting wind of that again, as I do every time he comes around to give a concert in Kent, has fueled these cool thoughts on our own, personal geography, and our own family romance of relationship across time.

I am not sure of its name, but it must be female. I mean that wind from the southwest that originates in Mexico, blows up across the high flat land across Texas and Oklahoma with very little to slow it down before it heats up Chicago, and whips on into Lake Superior in July or August. As I say, usually it is cool in the Upper Peninsula of Michigan but not when that wind blows up from the South. I am convinced that the women in my life have been like that wind, and I think my luminal movement to the north has been blown by that wind. Conversely, it may be the totem of the Big Lake itself that draws, or sucks, the wind and me north.

But long before I knew anything about the wind and, in fact, a decade before the Keweenaw in the Upper Peninsula even had telephones, my parents started renting a cottage at Old Homestead Beach a mile east of Huron on Lake Erie. The war was on, and no new tires were to be had and the gas was rationed. So we had to drive the eighty miles or so slowly with frequent stops for my Dad to patch and pump air into old rubber. Years later after both my parents were dead and I was happily into my second marriage, memory brought back what my mom had told me about my dad's marriage proposal to her on a crystal-clear, romantic lake in Michigan. That moment had been during the early Great Depression years, but to hear them tell it they must have felt like Wallis and the King of England. She was remembering and passing on to me family romance.

We are all commoners in America, however, and try to work to be cool, to avoid that hot wind from the South. But family romance generates our coolness always. I married first a Texas girl. My mom had been born in Oklahoma. The mother of the boys died the year of the American Bicentennial. By then I was teaching science fiction, and the following year I married again. My wife, who had dated her fellow Oklahoman the singer, had later married another singer, who did not want to stay married, and they had two girls. So our family romance blended, finally, in a marvelous symmetry. When my wife and I had the opportunity to buy our place far north, we did.

Last summer with the kids all grown and gone, we then at last made it out to the upper edge of the Big Lake, near the wide entrance to Keweenaw Bay. The Park Service boat we took, called the Ranger III, went out just a little way and then turned back into the channel. We had only signed up for the two-hour cruise. But at the turn, the lake stretched out, very large, gray and churning. This was much different from what I remembered of the Lake Erie beach near the breakwater rocks at Huron in Ohio. Though we only have a few black-and-white old photos from the 1940s, I see that time of war in my mind as soft and warm in color. Strangely, we are more or less at peace now, but the color has darkened some. And there is the wind.

In any case, my wife and I have now made the reservation so that next summer our plan is to go on the six-hour cruise out into the Big Lake and over to Isle Royale. So let this prose writing become a bridge to the borders and boundaries that link and separate the Big Lake and its smaller "great lakes" as well as our modes of telling and touching the story of family romance. In the meantime, I cannot convince my son the poet to visit us in upper Michigan with his own children. He thinks the place is haunted. He is probably right. With regard to Isle Royale, the Park Service says that moose have been seen swimming to it from the Canada side. I think we will feel bigger if we make it. This is one thing that the Great Lakes do for us, draw us across the bridges, the borders. I want always to be cool, of course; but I can proudly say that we are lucky folk—even if we never manage to make it to Mars. But finally, let me evoke my main hero from years ago but in his present day and very cool embodiment. The aging actor William Shatner played Captain James Kirk of the Starship *Enterprise* back when my small sons and I would watch the weekly shows amazed. Now Shatner sells for Travelocity on TV, and other younger actors do the *Star Trek* fantasies. But Shatner has a cool line that he delivers well as he stumbles overweight into the churning body of water, "We'll see where the waves take me."

Donald M. Hassler

Highway 61 and Beyond

Gina Genovese

I-35 cuts across the United States top to bottom—like a scar from open-heart surgery—from Laredo, Texas to Duluth, Minnesota, my hometown. There, it turns into Highway 61 of Bob Dylan fame—the scenic North Shore that hugs Lake Superior all the way up to Canada.

Duluth is filled with middle-class people largely of Scandinavian and German descent who attend church, vote, fish, and generally go about their lives without a lot of fuss or fanfare. Although located in the Midwest, Duluth is connected to the rest of the world by water that flows from Lake Superior—the rocky shores of which Duluth is built on—through the Saint Lawrence Seaway, and then out to the Atlantic, quietly, like us.

Bob Dylan was born in Duluth. His family lived in the top floor of a small house on the hill just a mile from the lake. He was born Robert Allen Zimmermann. "I don't remember much about Duluth, really, except, uh, the foghorns," he says. In interviews, he seems vaguely annoyed when asked about his Minnesota roots—like he's embarrassed by it, or by us. But still, I recognize home in his lyrics sometimes, bubbling up between the cracks, and I love him for it.

"I was born in, grew up in a place so foreign that you had to be there to picture it," he said once in a Playboy interview. "In the winter, everything was still, nothing moved. Eight months of that. There is a great spiritual quality throughout the Midwest. Very subtle, very strong, and that is where I grew up. New York was a dream."

The scenic North Shore drive is where people from the upper Midwest sometimes travel during those two weeks in September when the leaves give one last, brilliant hurrah before they loosen their grip and let go, and the lake turns an angry, vibrant blue. During these two weeks, any Minnesotan might feel that yes, yes, what we have here—it's something special. It's a breath from God. A gift from God, reminding us why we're here.

"Some people get born, you know, to the wrong names, wrong parents I mean, that happens. You call yourself what you want to call yourself. This is the land of the free," Dylan says.

But that feeling is short-lived. Soon the leaves let go and die, and the trees become skeletons, waving their bare arms in the wind, and the lake turns gray and the ice heaves—covering the frigid water with a blanket of snow where life somehow survives below it. And everyone sleeps. Sleeps and survives until the ice cracks six months later and the trout and the pike and the walleye and the geese and whitetail deer and the timber wolves and the black bear and the people—all of us—remember with a slowly beating heart that it's okay once again to wake up.

That's how it is there.

It's the winters that drove me away. Out to California, where the sun shone every day and people were better looking and somehow seemed to *know more*. Out west, where Dave Eggers went after his parents died, to start fresh. So I did too.

And still my mind often wanders to the gusty tip of Lake Superior, where December could be so cold that even time seemed to freeze—where the glare from the sun on the snow made me squint as I walked to my car, exhaling in short white puffs, snow crunching beneath my boots, keys clasped in mittened hands. Where icicles, like glass fingers, grasped tree branches—and where smoke from chimneys curled into the frosty sky before disappearing like snowflakes on a windshield or so many childhood dreams.

Ripe

Gwen Schwartz

Every year it was the same. And it was good. As in sweet, juicy goodness that made your stomach upset from eating too much. The ritual trip to Presque Isle after a morning of cherry picking in North East, Pennsylvania, just minutes from the beach. Well, not a real beach with ocean waves, but the beach at Presque Isle, on Lake Erie, just two hours north of my hometown.

I don't remember a year when I wasn't allowed up the ladders, holding a bucket into which very few cherries ever made a landing. There were years I was too small, years remembered by the faded pictures of me and my sister, Lisa, in yellow sun bonnets and matching bloomers under our sunflower dress-like tops. But of course I don't really remember those years; I remember the ones on the ladders, stretching out a hand for the perfect-looking deep red wonder. I ate so many cherries in the first hour of picking that I was actually able to concentrate on the job once my belly was all filled up: I knew that by the end of the morning, I had to produce a bucket for weighing, and my parents made a big deal of making sure we kids knew we had to have some heft to our buckets. We all had to do our part. But my brother, Josh, had different rules. Baby-of-the-family rules. Three years younger is a long time, and I didn't like it. Josh was allowed to climb the ladders at a younger age than I had been, and he still didn't have to fill up his bucket as much. But even as I still wish my parents had given him some responsibility, the memories left a permanent stain of sweetness on my tongue come the first week of July.

Families of today, from my hometown and elsewhere nearby, travel to Ocean Isle, North Carolina—like Presque Isle in name, but with a longer drive and with the reward of real ocean waves and saltwater fish, but without the cherries to pick before you arrive. Today we travel farther away because we can, because Lake Erie isn't good enough for us anymore. Maybe it wasn't ever good enough for some families, but for many, Lake Erie reminds us that we were deceived as kids.

I was a kid in the 1970s and Lake Erie was dirty by then. The rust belt had run into the water, and it was dying. It was unsafe for swimming, in fact, by some people's standards. And the dunes were shrinking. Not because of beach erosion, I was told, but because of overuse. Overuse of a dirty beach. Middle-class families without the means for fancy vacations flocked to Lake Erie, drove out to Presque Isle and chose among the limited number of parking spots right next to the road, trekked the picnic lunch or dinner packed in the old, wooden baskets up through the trees, over the dunes, and onto the luxurious, hot sand. Kids ran into the water, as wide and unburdened as the ocean must have been, oblivious to the fact that they were really just swimming in a very large lake. Oblivious to the smell of dead fish, dying waters, garbage, and human waste. To us, a day at the beach was one of the best days of summer. And not much was better than going to the beach when the cherries were ripe for picking.

Back then, cherries were well under a dollar a pound if you picked your own sweets. Sours were even less, according to my mother, who is like me and doesn't remember numbers. Mom's favorites were the sours, which she picked herself for a bunch of pies on the Fourth of July. She also canned cherries, in addition to tomatoes and peaches, so we'd have "fresh" food in the winter. I'm sad to say I mock my mother's canning now; canning she does to this day, now that I'm grown and have a family of my own and enough money to buy fresh produce year round. But my mother insisted that we kids learn how to be good at picking—probably for her practical need of cherries as much as for our development—so we picked cherries the right way, just like we learned how to pick out good shells at Presque Isle.

Shell picking is what I called it then, even though later I would learn that most people call it beachcombing. Like red cherry stained memories, the pungent scent of Erie that suffocated Dad's and my long walks along the beach where we would pick up shells left a smell in my mind that was recently (and instantly) recalled when my family went to the beach at Presque Isle for an afternoon of relaxation after my husband ran the Erie marathon. That smell is very present, so I was amazed when my kids didn't seem to notice it. It gave me an appreciation for my parents' willingness to take us to the beach in spite of it; it also made me wonder about the safety of the water.

A year before I was born, Presque Isle was named a National Natural Landmark by the National Park Service. My folks were big into camping our way across the country, so this news must have, in part, launched our family trips to the Lake Erie area. My mother tells me that we went cherry picking because there was an ad in the *Pittsburgh Press* and she liked cherries, so a trip was planned. None of this was known to me at the time, nor would it have mattered. What did matter were the shells and the sand. In my yellow rubber swimming cap with its white rubber daisies sticking out every which way, I ran onto the sand and plunked myself down with my little plastic shovel and the requisite sand bucket. But unlike the cherry-picking bucket, which was slow to fill up, my sand pail would quickly fill with what I considered to be the most beautiful shells on earth. Of course I hadn't been to an ocean yet, so I hadn't met the conch or the whelk yet, but still, I was pleased with pebbles of varying shades of amber.

There is a healing rhythm to the beach, regardless of its smell or its health, regardless of the beach you go to. When I was a kid, we went to Beach 9 or 10 at Presque Isle, popular but not overcrowded on a hot July afternoon. Today, you can get free loaner beach wheelchairs at the Yellow Bike Shop, and Beach 7 has a wheelchair ramp to the beach. That where we'd take our niece, Sarah, if her family ever visited us in Ohio, or our nephew Noah, if he were still living and we wanted a family getaway closer than our traditional week at Ocean Isle. I'm both amazed and relieved that so many activities that were shut off to physically limited people for so long are now more accessible. I don't ever remember a wheelchair on a beach when I was a kid, but then again, the jogger stroller hadn't even been invented yet. My sister and her husband pushed Noah in his jogger at the beach in North Carolina for each of the four years he lived, and even though we won't ever really know if he experienced delight at the seagulls or awe at the waves, the beach, and the wind, they held his attention.

The beach has a way of holding our attention for long stretches of time. When my kids are at the beach, their attention is captured by the impossible: building a castle with a moat that will not be destroyed by the waves. While some kids might choose the safe route and build far up on the beach, Julia and Jordan are more daring. They like to tempt the waves. Once the castle and the moat are done, they need to be decorated, which means we must search for shells. And when one needs shells that are good, some long-ago lesson in cherry picking comes in handy: go slowly. Don't reach too far beyond where you are perched, whether on a ladder or on the sand; after all, you never know what might lurk just under the sand's surface, dangerous and shiny, the glass of a beer bottle just waiting to tetanus your day. Once you find a shell, turn it over, slowly. There is always the chance of something gross and nasty.

You have to be careful—methodical—like an engineer, really. Stake out a quadrant, mark it off in your mind, just like you'd stake out a tree and pick one limb completely before moving on to another, lower down (because the higher limbs are always the most fun to pick and the farthest away from little brother, who couldn't reach as high and therefore didn't get the "best" cherries). On the beach, the higher-up shells are hard to find; they've already been beachcombed by the old people who time the ebb and flow of shell washup just right. So you have to rely on the lower limbs of the beach, in the wet sand near the edge of the water, where the puny waves curl around your heels and sink you ankle-deep into black or green mud, depending on the beach and the time of year.

The shells are slick and shimmery, and they seem to have colors that the higher-up ones do not. Their rounded edges suggest that the waves here at Presque Isle have the same effect as ocean waves, smoothing roughness into wind and water-swept sweeping contours, like what you might see just outside Zion National Park, when you're older, and you call the rock formations "cow paddy meadow" because of their smooth, paddy-like windswept sandstone shape. The smooth, small shells are perfect for castle decorating. They are not brilliant; they are common, and in their country calmness, they give the kids abundant resources for their building adventure.

We play at Presque Isle until the sun dips; we have a two-and-a-half-hour drive to get back to our home in Ohio, and we have work the next day. We towel off, pack up, walk out, load up, and take Peninsula Drive back past the rest of the beaches, out to West 12th Street and back to I-79, south to I-80 and west to Alliance, home. Presque Isle stays with us in the car. We're sand-soaked and sticky, just like I was as a child, riding home in my parents' old blue Chevy. We don't have the cherry stains of my youth, but the kids have the sand in their memories and in their Keens, and they too will be able to smell the Lake, years into the future, when their kids want a day at the beach. The smell will not be what it is really, which is really quite nasty; rather, it will be the smell of sunscreen (not suntan lotion, as it was in the 1970s) and water fowl, green-smelling water and the Doritos from lunch. Presque Isle, all eleven miles of its beaches, is one of those places that linger in the memory as the best beach there is. At least until you go to the ocean.

Cherries are still available near Lake Erie today, even though they cost a buck and a quarter to pick a pound. And this past summer, said one of the Boyce Farms owners, there was a very small harvest because of the draught. The fruit belt, as it's called, is alive and well, though, even if the Lake isn't. Welch's continues its booming grape business and new products are added yearly to its line of famous grape juices. Wineries have even become prosperous in the region. And, while the EPA has implemented a number of restrictions on waste and runoff, problems continue. Phosphorous runs off from the farms' fertilizers and green algae plagues certain areas in the late summer. People are taking notice, though. The Lake's contamination is studied carefully by those invited to The Great Lakes Summit in Cleveland. They even certify beaches safe for swimming when the water toxins are below an agreed-upon number. You can get updates through an app on your phone. We've come a long way. I'd rather travel farther, though, and sit on a clean beach whose waters are not questionable. Castles aside, I'd rather remember the sweet sticky from cherry picking rather than the ripeness of the Lake.

Selected Poems by D.E. Green

D.E. Green

Temperance River

Urbanity never knows quite
what to make of nature,
comes with *Blue Guide* visions
Cascading into Superior,
mosquitoes worrying the hearty hardy—
ghosts of old explorers, Saturday pioneers—
who expect the Look-Out's pay-off
and get what they expect.

So do we consume nature's sites,
broker this green world,
market its magnificence,
label its goods.

But sometimes nature mocks preconception,
startles expectation with astounding modesty:
though we can marvel at white waters gorging,
we must *feel* what (hidden) carves its outlet,
conceals its bubbling force in cauldrons,
works (abashedly) its ways out of view—
tempering with restraint its power.

Pantoum: The Western Sky

Clouds loom over Chicago and the western sky.
Michigan's waters calm my nerves,
jangled by traffic and road construction.
I float belly-up and watch the circling gulls.

Michigan's waters calm my nerves.
The Lake swells gently, soothes me with its liquid sighs.
I float belly-up and watch the circling gulls.
They remind me of the voraciousness I've left behind.

The Lake swells gently, soothes me with its liquid sighs.
The sky's blue colors my thoughts a limpid azure.
They remind me of the voraciousness I've left behind—
Those gulls swooping and crying over head.

The sky's blue colors my thoughts a limpid azure.
I shut my eyes, rock to the waves, shut out the world.
Those gulls swooping and crying over head—
how can we satisfy such hunger?

I shut my eyes, rock to the waves, shut out the world
jangled by traffic and road construction.
How can we satisfy such hunger?
Clouds loom over Chicago and the western sky.

Loons

The loons are at it again
In the middle of the night
Hooting and quarreling,

Moaning their joy and pain,
Cawing commands,
Shrieking like Shakespearean shrews.

I wake, worry the sheets,
Toss off the twisted covers,
Turn, slip under again—

Sleeping on edge, awaiting
Again the loons' shrill keening.

D.E. Green

Northern Winter

Here in the northland, night's shadow lengthens
into light. On warm winter days snow-clad
eaves metamorphose drop by drop into the clear
cold fangs of darkness. Night is always near.

The solstitial chill feeds on snow's reflected
light. Cardinals, redder than remembrance,
fly—silent simulacra of the living,
vermilion life surviving on the wing.

On coldest days searing blue light abounds,
arises everywhere, blinds every creature—
as cruel to sight as to the eye the razor's edge.
Icicles and snow pack crack, acknowledge

winter's dominion. Dull cold shadow of life,
earth holds its breath still, still, for spring's green strife.

Grain Elevator

The traffic on Hiawatha
(Backdoor to the city)
Always stalls by the ADM
Elevator, trucks backed in
To load and cart the grain away.

Today I'm waiting at the light
And notice under the mammoth
Cylinders Sheeler immortalized
A small spill, a hillock of corn—
Never to be planted, boiled, or popped.

But it is already nourishing
The sparrows, a small flock
Whirling over our windshields
To land on the curbless drive
By the elevator's loading dock.

They scratch and pick,
Peck and nibble at the pile.
Each sparrow does its part.
The little mound collapses,
its elements lifted skyward.

We watch because we cannot
Move, because this little fracas
Mirrors our own small worlds,
Our immediate destinations,
Our tussle over others' leavings.

When the light changes
We look away, ease forward.
We are on our way,
Mindless of sparrows
Wheeling overhead.

D.E. Green

Chicago Heat

When it's 90-something in Chicago,
the breeze off the Lake gives scant relief.
Joggers and strollers rain perspiration.
In the fountains at Millenium Park,
the children splash and scream.

But on Michigan they're shooting the seventh
sequel to a bad disaster flick: At Wacker
the drawbridge is frozen open. Cars are in flames.
A helicopter shoots it all from above.

Citizens are dropping of sunstroke.
But that's no disaster:
We got to see 'em blow up Mickey Rourke.

In Old Beloit

Thunder—low, rumbling, persistent.
Suddenly, a gust turned gale
rains down on them a flood
of flying bugs—the kind
that dance in the streetlights
along the river walk in old Beloit.

D.E. Green

I Go, You Stay

Blair Bohland

I picked the school for the colors. I liked the richness of the burgundy and the warmth of the gold. It was my first college tour, and I was in love. How could I not be—a school as beautiful as this? And I could live here and study here and read and write? This school was what I had been planning for. Then we were shown through the next building, the walk feeling longer than it was. It was cold, which wasn't a surprise. I was in Chicago, and I hadn't been here before. From Ohio I understood the cold—and the wind, to a certain extent—but this was a different kind of wind, an incessant stinging that refused to leave, even in the warmth of a library.

Disregarding the biting at my skin, I couldn't keep my eyes off the lake. It was right there, in the library, or at least it seemed to be. The massive body of water hid between the aisle ways of books (how it managed to fit between them, I don't know) and emerged in large, thrashing spans of glass. In front of the window, students sat studying at various tables, unaware of the harsh gray slapping the short bluff of rocks. Most of the students had multiple books spanned across their tables, others had headphones in, and a few were wasting away at their phones. Perhaps the students had become spoiled from frequent visitation, or had become indifferent due to the distractions of their own lives. But the lake! It had its own life, too. And now it matched the wind's fury, and my vision of a serene, still lake—a lake I had never seen before—vanished, replaced instead by the icy turmoil outside this library window.

I grew up by the ocean, but hadn't seen a lake. I imagined them to be unmoving and glassy: the epitome of calm—certainly, not *this*. I couldn't help but long for the feeling of the lake. My life was as the neatly structured Dewey-Decimaled shelves of books; I could write out a seven-year plan I had for myself in about five minutes. Unfortunately, I was also only seventeen.

I wondered how many of the students inside this library had really taken the time to appreciate the water, the water that was right next to them every day. Completely stop, put down their electronics (and yes, even books), and look at the water. *Feel* the water. But I suppose that's how we work in our world, forced to be constantly progressing, constantly moving, constantly finding a way to do more, be more, and do it all more quickly, more efficiently. At times I so badly wished to be the lake, I became even more depressed in my human body. Don't misunderstand my intention— I admired humanity—but many times we seemed so selfish, so earthly in the most negative sense of the word. Hardly an hour a day was taken away from some form of an electronic, or anything that was a reminder of the modern world we live in. I spent all day every day, planning my life, tiptoeing around my friends and my family and strangers...all to avoid displeasing them in any way...and all for the ultimate goal of being structured, being an outstanding or impressive—coveted—citizen. But what use was it, really? What use were forty-thousand-dollar tuitions and constant games of charades we play to peacock those around us? None, when it took me further and further from my roots, from the peaceful and fulfilling existence of nature.

And *that* is why I am jealous of the lake. I'm jealous because I want to be it—I want to just be. Yes, the lake also meant turmoil, and uncertainty, but I would gladly trade my societal turmoil for the turmoil of the lake. Even in being imperfect the lake is perfect since it is nature, because it does not judge and cannot know judgment. It is so magnanimously perfect, it is nearly self-sacrificial. Every day we live, the water takes the stress and scum of humanity and swirls it downstream, so it can bathe in our sin and suffer our consequences. Our being what we are makes the lake pure, a messiah of our everyday sins, washing away worry with a simple look over its surface.

And I was envious. I wanted to be perfect, to be as sinless and beautiful and one with nature as the lake itself is. But I knew it was impossible. I could only look and want and admire the lake even more, knowing I could never possibly achieve what the water could, and return to my chaotic human life.

She let us walk outside, the tour guide did. There was a thin strip of sidewalk between the outside building wall and steep decline into the waters. She pulled in her coat and walked quickly. I snuck in a quick rub across my nose with my sleeve, picking up the trailing snot efficiently, before she turned back to make sure we— my mom and I—were still responsive. I couldn't hear much of what our guide was saying. I kept my hood up, despite this inability, and grabbed at the flying strands of my hair. We would have to leave for the next building soon, unless someone asked a question we couldn't hear the answer to. But they didn't and we kept walking. I turned my head back for a last glimpse of the rugged water. At first the way it so recklessly threw itself against the rock made me worry, but really the lake was doing what it was doing. It was just being. And with that thought, I felt calmer.

On the way home I thought of the students in the library, books piled and opened on the desks, wrapped tightly in warmth and filled with knowledge, while the lake beat right there at the window. This was my only thought, rather sluggish and mundane. I watched the green signs fly by down the highway, bits of trash and tire and tree scattered down the interstate. I couldn't see the lake. And so we left.

Blair Bohland

Isle Royale

Karl Elder

Monday, June 23rd

It's 5:00 p.m. I sit with gloves on at a picnic table. Camp is set; the red squirrels are omnipresent. I guard the steaks while Seth reads in our tent and the others have taken off to the pier at the bottom of the trail.

Three Mile is what they call this site. There's another troop up the hill a bit, the leader of which fell (on slippery rock?) and hurt his knee, elbow, and head. On the same trail a few roads after that accident, we ran into a fox, sitting on its haunches. The kids dropped their packs to retrieve their disposable cameras.

It's raining, has rained—off and on—since we arrived on the island. Had rain on the ferry, too, a rough ride. Mr. Ertman tossed his doughnuts, but as far as I could tell, nobody else got sick on the boat.

"Group 9," our troop's other half, apparently had trouble getting completely packed at the lodge. Myron just told one of our boys that the group left—to Daisy Farm—about an hour after us. Passing us, they still have a ways to go to land a site.

Tuesday, June 24th, 6:30 a.m.

I slept well and warm, the first to get out of bed, as I was the last to go to bed. Such is easier on my back.

Karl Elder

There's fog. There's always fog, it seems. Birds call, and moose dung litters the trail to the latrine. It's funny that by appearance the dung has no sign of age—anywhere. The moose could have been here a moment ago or a month ago. There's a good deal of gravel-like dark rock on the trail that also lends the illusion of being petrified moose droppings.

Our campsite—it's rather huge—stretches along a 15-feet-high cliff. It's really gorgeous, the moss here and there on these irregular-shaped bales of stone stacked as if in a loft, gray bales, of course, like an enormous stone mural to look upon, like a giant's stone steps that the kids climb in one area, immediately over my right shoulder. I haven't so much as left this spot to go to the shore for water, sending the kids instead. Why walk about when one has here one's space and shadows to search on the foundation of a cathedral? Part of what makes the site seem so wide is the narrowness of the trails, I suppose, vistas stretching off into more wild like caves in the side of wilderness. Black and gray and green and brown. No blue. No yellow, with the exception of wildflowers at the bottom of the cliff. And red? The only red today, I remember, I saw after swatting a mosquito. Yes, they're here, even at 7:00 a.m.

*Wednesday, June 25*th

It's 8:00 p.m.; we've got a group site at Lake Richie. It's dry. Yesterday was wet. Oceanic. A ranger told us it was the season's big rain. We got hit with rain on the trail yesterday, just outside of Daisy Farm. I tried to get us to shelter, knowing that we were close, but I called for a halt by a stand of trees just short of one of the buildings obscured by vegetation. We moved on and found an empty shelter, the first of four, and it easily accommodated us all—eight—for lunch.

Then the rain stopped. We moved on toward Moskey Basin and were dry for a while until, shortly, during a break, it became clear that the clouds were about to dump on us again. It rained. It rained. It rained until midnight. We were miserable, unpacking, setting up, cooking, and trying to sleep. Jeff S. sacrificed his sleeping bag— rather, himself—to a cold, sleepless night. (Jerod's had gotten soaked.) Jeff and I were up at about 5:00, working to get things dry again. We carried tents out several yards to a stone point, dunked tarps in the lake, etc. It took six hours, and it's a good thing we had only 2.5 or so miles to hike today. We started out at about 2:30, made 2.1 miles in exactly forty-five minutes. Then we searched for our current site.

The kids—younger ones—jumped in the lake early this morning. I stripped and took a sponge bath, which wasn't all that unpleasant, thanks to the water's temperature in the middle of the cove. Wade dunked his head, washed, but wouldn't strip. I saw that Jeff was wet; he and others were by one of the shelters, cleaning up.

As might be expected, the adults—including Seth—seem to have assumed the lion's share of work. Jeff is the technical expert. He keeps the stoves operating and the "good water" flowing from the pump. He's exhausted. Seth is a horse, as usual on these trips. He carries a lot and sometimes sets the pace when we hike, a pace which is too great for Jeff and me, so I usually lead; I'm more cautious and have slipped several times but not fallen. Seth actually fell on the rain trail (I guess Ghram caught him). Me, I have the bag (pack) full of tricks, which sometimes lightens the load, like needle-nose pliers for missing hot pot tongs. I pump water and have made a few executive decisions. It's a good leadership team.

I remember that I awoke on the morning of the big rain before the others. I walked down to the lapping and gurgling shore with the water pail, surprised to see fog on the lake. Dipping the bucket, letting the water trickle into it, suddenly I could not tell its sound from that of a loon and, looking up, there it was, a loon, but a few feet away, calling out. Stepping back, it occurred to me how effortless it is, moving into the next moment of my life. I took the trail one step at a time, mostly, for the entire day. It is not that I want this to end. And I'm glad it's begun, that, finally I'm here, after so much preparation. The end will come soon enough. I'm just trying to live this, to think a bit, to experience the moods and emotions, the rain and the sun, but not in that order, necessarily. We eat well, but I have a craving for Diet Coke. I have my tobacco. Some coffee.

Birds flirt with us all day. Woodpeckers, orioles, sparrows, ducks, loons, and many whose species I do not know. There's one particularly sweet songbird whose mate echoes from far off, I assume. The sound is as pleasant as many of the smells—fragrant, fresh, and omnipresent.

Coming out of our shelter at lunch from Daisy Farm, headed up the trail, Jerod said, "I'd know that laugh anywhere; that's Mr. Ertman!"

Indeed, through the trees we could see him, and then was revealed "Group 9's" campsite. We yelled something about them getting up so late, not having yet hit the trail, when Mr. Ertman cried, "Karl, I've got to tell you something. Wait up ."

Then, what the boys jokingly call "the honeymoon couple," tent mates Nate and J.C., who are each rather territorial, appeared, Nate instantly alleviating the small jolt of fear at Mr. Ertman's words, calling from afar, "It wasn't too bad, but something happened." Matt, according to Mr. Ertman, blew out his knee on the first day. He couldn't put weight on it. So they would be "stuck" at Daisy Farm. Nate, not given to discretion, inhibition, or pride, confided with all in our group, slipping from one person to the other, whispering that he was glad that his group wouldn't have to "walk" anymore, although, of course, he added, he wasn't glad for poor Matt. Lounging all week at Daisy Farm on Isle Royale! The life!

A volunteer apparently told Mr. Ertman that they—Isle Royale rangers—would try to accommodate Group 9 since the census wasn't real high yet, it being early in the season. They, Group 9, will hike back to Three Mile, camp, and finally return Saturday morning to Rock Harbor to catch the ferry. They tell us they want us there on Saturday morning at 10:30 from 7 miles away at Daisy Farm. Good luck. We'll have to wake very, very early, already packed, snack on the trail, and keep Seth in the lead to pace us.

Thursday, June 26th, 11:15 a.m.

Have eaten lunch on Chicken Bone West Lake. Lots of hills this morning. The last one was a killer, about three-fifths of the height of the big sand dune at Warren Dunes. We make great time with Seth pacing us. We're pumping water, fishing, eating, and looking at the map. Only 2.7 miles yet to go today, along the lake, so it should be cool.

Ran into a moose skeleton with the skull missing this morning and saw a beautiful print in the black peat. Walking over 2 x 8 boards in one swamp was like stepping into a Georgia O'Keeffe painting. The swamp was dominated by gargantuan leaves of something like rhubarb, their texture like red-green elephant hide.

Ryan just caught a northern pike—16 inches, maybe, our first fish, 11:25 a.m.

Thursday, 7:35 p.m.

"Telling great stories now," Jerod says, a kind of mantra. I suppose he's mocking my journal.

The trail from West Chicken Bone was entirely along the lake. We saw plenty of signs of beaver but no beaver. Traveled hard, pushed ourselves, and stopped a half mile before the group sites. We had three sites from which to choose; we rejected the first one, although it's near, just over a ridge. We got a site with some—but little—shade and set up the tarp with difficulty. It was warm, too warm. We're surrounded by paper birches, which aren't fully bloomed—the white birches are. There are daises. I took some pictures using a variety of lenses and the Polaroid filter. I look forward to seeing them developed. (I tried a couple of new things.) Seth is reading *Absolute Power*. He and Wade returned only a short while ago from the lake, having cleaned up. Jeff and I spent some time at the picnic table talking about the curse of being managers back home and the character of some of the kids our sons hang out with. Soon all the kids were here and reliving funny movies. "Telling great stories now," Jerod said. Could the expression be out of a movie I missed?

Friday, June 27th, 7:12 p.m.

Today was a challenge to match the largest of all days except for a couple spent in the army and in the Boundary Waters.

Awoke at 5:00 a.m. with sunlight streaming over the horizon directly into the door of the tent, my head there to ward off Seth's snores, which peaked at about five on the Richter scale at odd moments during the night. (I opened my eyes several times, checking the weather. All clear, with stars, complete.)

Anyway, my first thought upon waking was to catch a shot of the sunrise, including our site. I raced and lost. The dang camera failed again. Again today. It obviously will require repair. And such a marvelous set of pictures I missed. Compositions like that through the viewfinder I haven't seen for years.

Something called for an omelet for breakfast after I trekked to the lake for water and boiled it for coffee and later packed, laboriously. Everyone seemed caught in slow motion, but finally we left, 8:30. Immediately after passing a gorgeous waterfall on a brook, we began our ascent. About 2 miles to Chicken Bone East where a guy (from another group with whom we seemed to play leap frog) informed us that the worst was still to come. I thought of Group 9, wondering how some of its members, younger boys than ours, could have possibly made it even as far as we'd come, and we hadn't begun to tackle the ridge, which was another 200 feet up in elevation. How could we know that the next 5.5 miles would be like an ascent into the inferno, as hot as it gets up there with no water source? Oh, we had filled our canteens, but some of us were out of water by half way. I passed ibuprofen to Jeff, swallowed a couple tablets myself at the two-mile marker, and continued to climb. It was like stairs in some spots, steep stairs. And we climbed and climbed and climbed with forty to fifty pounds digging into our shoulders and hips.

I think I began to get delirious. I couldn't stop, I was so tired, so I led for a while—till lunch at about 10:45, although, since we had so little water, we ate only dried pineapple rings and granola bars, which served to make us thirstier. We, while resting in shade, saw a solitary approaching woman, with a sturdy staff like Mr. Ertman's.

She appeared a bit apprehensive coming upon us as it was as if we were a wolf pack crouched on both sides of the path, ready to spring. If only she knew how tired we were. I called "hello" to her a half dozen yards before she would make it to us through patches of sunlight, and that seemed to relieve the tension on her face. One of the kids asked her where she had begun this morning and how long ago; she said that she'd started at 8:00 but that she typically does a lot of "dorking around." I have her pegged for an educator. She's a Troop Committee Chair, we came to discover. Quite self-reliant, attractive, in her early forties, I'd say, and, after she had decided to push on, having told us where she'd been, I said to her, seeing the patch on her back, "You've been to Philmont, huh?"

She turned to face me and held up three fingers. "You guys must be a troop," she said, and she started talking. She's from Viking Council, forty miles north of the Twin Cities in Minnesota.

So now Seth would be in the lead—bad for me but good for making time. Finally, after climbing another, god-awful hill, looking upon another incredible view toward the far side of the island, we rested shortly and then pushed on to an intersection, which would lead us to Daisy Farm, where we now camp, not having set much up because of the pressure on us to make 7.5 miles in the morning before 10:30. At the intersection, I heard Eliot say that he'd give just about anything for another drink of water, so I, in a while, gave him a swig, not realizing others were also out of water.

Me, I had about ten swallows left, I figured, and I was determined to save the rest for emergencies—should there be any—or at least the last 1.9 miles, which, as the kids say, was a "long" 1.9. I agree. I think the rangers must have miscalculated when they erected the mile marker.

I had no idea I would fall so far behind. I thought, since we were on the ridge, that the rest of the walk would be downhill to Superior and Daisy Farm. Foolish me. I stopped to urinate, could no longer see a backpack ahead of me, and when I came upon a valley with boardwalk stretching completely across it, a couple hundred yards long, it was only me and Mother Nature.

And there were these wonderful sights. A strange hidden lake and beautiful wild irises stuck in the marsh every so often— tempting, all, tempting to slow down, and then it dawned on me that valley implies hill. Shit.

Later I heard up ahead that Ghram did.

Well, Jeff had lingered, waiting for—he thought—Wade and me—so I caught up with him, barely able to decipher what he was saying about "young bucks" up ahead. "Ain't no deer here," I said to myself and then realized what he meant was the he too was laboring, his heart, he said, beating too fast for too long. We struggled on. I thought we'd taken the path to infinity, my pack now three times as heavy as when we began as I cursed rock, root, wood, mud, thinking where the hell is that marker? When we hit it, Jeff lit up. He thought we had another 1.7 miles to go, having not realized that we were off the ridge! That's how strange that "downhill" trail was. Indeed the mile marker said 0.2 miles to Daisy Farm on the back side. Jeff was confused at first, and I swear that one of the oddest thoughts I've had in my life is the notion of a man, in total shock—surprised—doing a jig with a fifty-pound pack on his back and a pair of fishing rods duct taped to a dinning fly pole in his hand.

In the back of my mind all the while was Seth, who I feared might suffer heat stroke or something like it, given his diabetes. When we came—Jeff and I—onto the first group site, there sat Seth—in the sun no less! "We've got to have shade!" I yelled.

Seth turned his head and said, "I dumped my pack on the first picnic table I saw."

We took site 3, the site of the honeymooners.

Seth dragged himself up the hill, low blood sugar and all. "Got any of that candy?" he asked, and Jeff—I believe—thought Seth was kidding. It was no joke. He immediately chewed two pieces of hard candy I gave him, saying that his legs were barely carrying him up the last hill to our site. We pumped more sugar into him, and he lay on an air mattress and slept for an hour.

(A fox just stole Ghram's toothbrush and toothpaste out of his pack.)

Actually, we got here early in the day and unpacked little—certainly not the tents for fear that they might get wet and weighty—in preparation for our forced march in the morning. I hope to sleep under the stars, but others have taken off to claim shelters, two of the four buildings empty.

[Two days later, home]

I slept under faded stars, alone, about a quarter mile from the rest of the group—the five kids in one shelter and Jeff and Seth in another.

Clouds—gauzy clouds—began to drift overhead at 11:30 p.m., which hid the moon through my binoculars.

Took me a long while to get to bed, hanging stuff in trees so critters couldn't get to it and doing so in the dark. There were a few mosquitos, but I'd figured it wouldn't be bad because of a weather forecast I'd heard earlier from a guy and his two sons downhill on shore. What I mean is that I'd anticipated the breeze would keep bugs at bay, probably. There was in the distance lightning, although I strained to hear thunder. I awoke to one gust that forced my poncho, which I'd secured over my backpack, to levitate for an instant, and then this stand of a dozen huge birches to my left seemed to inhale and exhale fitfully all night. It was sort of like being in the tent with Seth. Except that he is much louder.

I drank several sips of water and had to get up twice in the night. Now, at 3:50, I was wide awake. I rose for the last time and began packing when, ten minutes later, Jeff appeared to materialize out of the dark to pick up a bunch of equipment and awaken me for our hike back to Rock Harbor to meet our other group for the boat ride to Copper Harbor. We would eat on the pier, Jeff decided, to avoid the bugs. Fine with me. Forty minutes later I still wasn't completely packed, fumbling, hunting duct tape for blisters, only to conclude somebody had used my last.

By around 6:30 we were eating, many of us in a foul mood, dreading the 7.5-mile hike we needed to make quick, even though we realized the terrain would be flat. But not smooth, which can have a considerable "impact" upon blistered feet. Wade now complained of a sore heel, and he dug at us all to get us going. He wanted it all to be over with, the burning of the blister, that is.

There's little to explain the rate at which the group moved other than to say we were hiking in the cool of the day along a lake that, according to the boater I'd spoken with the night before, was at forty-four degrees. Of course, we were lighter, too, having consumed most of the food and fuel. In other words, we flew, Jeff and I in back, unable at times to see the kids ahead. Seth subsequently told me that he put, of all people, Wade, in the lead at the last. Wade, who, now, suddenly had a kick that carried him across the finish line and pulled the other boys with him in record time. I know what was on Wade's mind—the island store and its refrigerator, loaded with soda, although I later about choked on mine, shelling out for drinks for all, a 20-percent surcharge attached to anything purchased from a private vendor around the lodge area.

I sipped my Diet Coke alone, focusing south, far beyond the harbor onto the keen edge of the great expanse of slate-black water called Superior that, lost even to its surface, could kill a person with

its cold temperature in five minutes. I thought for a moment about
civilization and the morning's breakneck pace back to the dull
divide between it and wilderness. Was it the caffeine? The
ibuprofen? Suddenly the blisters didn't burn so bad.

Our Wine Dark Seas

Holly Lynn Baumgartner

Homer's *Iliad* begins with the memorable word "Rage." Both the Iliad and the Odyssey are sea stories and have generated some of the most potent water images in the Western Tradition, like the iconic metaphor of "the wine-dark sea." Yet Homeric force is a legacy of the Great Lakes, too, these ancient inland seas spinning their own haunting tales of heroes and horrors.

And so, any lover of these Midwestern oases recognizes their Janus faces and comes to intimately understand that "Great" is not a reference to "okay" as in "great, let's go," nor a reference to "large", but more like "Oz, the Great and Terrible" where no man, only Mother Nature, is behind the curtain.

I grew up on the Lakes, and the first song I was taught was not the song of Achilles nor even a Kindergarten standby like "I'm a Little Teapot." My first song was "The Wreck of the Edmund Fitzgerald," which gave me nightmares for weeks, and, still to this day, a particularly nasty storm rolling in over the lake will raise up from my mental depths, unbidden, Lightfoot's lyrics to the surface waters of memory.

My father's cousin drowned at Reno Beach, kids swimming in what should have been a protective bay: one gone missing. That bit of family lore was never talked about above a whisper, even by the time I was born. "The lake it is said, never gives up her dead" is an adage applying to all the Great Lakes, not just Superior. With a surface area of 94,250 square miles, the Lakes embrace quite a death toll, more than thirty thousand souls. However, these were simply stories to me, and only when I began to be a character in them myself did I learn that the site of pennant-streaming boat parades, of rowboat races and wave-runner surfing, of life-sustaining summer suppers, is also the site of primal fear, of darkness, of drowning.

My first real adventure was semi-comic at its start. The open waters and the busy bays are one of the last (somewhat) unregulated havens. There is something quintessentially American about the Lakes—no safety belts nor speed limits—just wide, beckoning, blue-gray road. After the heady freedom of a Lake Erie crossing, my family had moored at Put-in-Bay Island for a long weekend, perhaps Labor Day before everyone closes up shop and boats are tucked into drydock for wicked Ohio and Michigan winters. As a child, I loved these sailor's evenings of the long dusk, the ripples breaking the island lights into dancing swathes of color. Boats were tied together, five to six at a time, with the resulting bridge of decks a potent teaching tool. You never knew who might climb across your stern or, conversely, what you might see crossing someone else's—it was very educational.

On some nights, garbage can dinners brought my *Stone Soup* storybook alive, as everything from corn and cabbage to chicken and shellfish or a healthy dose of beer was tossed into a gray metal bin with its cymbal clashing topper, then propped up on cinder blocks over an open fire. When the lids were lifted, the seemingly endless bounty materialized out of the steam performing the small miracle of feeding the five hundred paper-plate-carrying boaters and their families and any other visitors who stumbled onto the docks with empty hands. It was my first lesson in community, even more than church; all were welcome and none went empty-handed.

As always, we ended our weekend with pizza at Frosty's, where they loaded on the cheese, each slice a mountain of fragrant goo. Of course, I ate too much, especially after devouring an entire pickle selected from the glass jars lining the bar while we waited for lunch to arrive. The breeze was picking up as we left, and friends cautioned against leaving. My dad was experienced and confident we could outrun the storm. I knew he would never put us in danger, and my blithe childish ignorance translates into even greater confidence in his choice as an adult looking back, aware now of his own encounters with lakes and loss.

The winds kicked up a tempest of whitecaps out over the lake, and the flying bridge tilted ominously like a sailboat before the wind, but our Chris-Craft cabin cruiser was no sailboat. Still, ballast held true, snapping us upright again, only to have the choppy waves pitch us in the other direction. Our mother finally ordered my sister and me into the forecabin, latching the door behind her when she left. As the boat keeled treacherously on her sides, we were thrown across the connected beds right up the slanting walls and on top of the portholes, which were under water until we rolled back and up the other wall, mimicking the heaving of the boat. Tossed like a child's teddy bear, we laughed hysterically at the crazy carnival ride. It was better than the inflatable bouncy tents of Bay View's Homecoming festival because the boat did our jumping for us. Then it hit.

Not the storm. The nausea. We vomited up chunks of Frosty's cheese and streams of sauce, leaving trails to mark our path. The violent rocking aided in projection until the walls ran red. When our mother opened the door, she screamed in terror even as the boat finally gentled into the Maumee River and safety. She thought we had been bounced to a bloody pulp. It was a long time before I could face pizza again. Later, scoured down—both boat and children— and exhausted, we battened the hatches to ride out the storm at dock. Its viciousness left us bruised and numb by the gray-streaked morning.

A clanging bell that was all alarm roused us and we raced with others round to the opposite side of the docks where a Coast Guard tug was tying up. One guardsman led a blanket-wrapped woman off across a hastily thrown plank, her wild, frizzy hair framing a slack mouth and empty eyes. She was the palest person I had ever seen, but it was her eyes that unnerved me. My dad directed us quickly away, but I hung back, demanding, "What's wrong with her?" They hushed me, but I, who never argued, would not be silenced. "What's wrong with her face?"

"She's in shock," my mom said finally. I tasted this new word gingerly. I did not like it.

"They shouldn't have tried it," my dad muttered grimly, shaking his head. The Coast Guard had not managed to save anyone else aboard the vessel that had started back too late to beat the storm. That night I dreamed of the little fore bedroom filling with mottled green water, felt the cold ferocity of its clutching fingers, and saw again her face at the porthole, dead eyes focused on nothing external in a body still alive.

Sometimes I imagine the Lakes like killing fields, with thousands of tide-bleached bones poking up out of the rocky bottoms This is my counter story balancing out everything I love tied to the Lakes:

Hiking the Sleeping Bear sand dunes for hours until I suddenly stumble from the last stark and sandy corridor to find the lake stretching like an ocean before me

Gathering Petoskey Stones on a sharp and tangled shore

Eating ice cream on Mackinac while sitting on comber-smoothed rocks, tidal pools washing my feet in blessing

Staring out over the Lake from the top of a Cedar Point roller coaster, when the fall from the top seems to last forever...

Poseidon may not stir these depths—they are far too Indian for that—but Homer would have felt at home among the heroics and horrors of Great Lakes deaths, when life and light are swallowed up by the enraged waters of our own wine-dark seas.

An Unmatched Fishing Trip

William J. Vande Kopple

"But it's about eight hours away!"

"Ah, come on. Do you ever listen to yourself? It's a bit of a drive up there, sure, but no way it's eight hours."

My friend Arnie and I were making the moves in a mainly-for-fun argument that we had been through dozens of times in the past.

It always started the same way. I would recount for him—in a tone apparently too close to boastful for his taste—what I regarded as unmatched fishing success on a recent wading excursion on the Flat River near Lowell.

"You should have seen them," my voice was almost an octave above normal. "Five thick beauties. Five smallmouth, all about twenty inches long. And they all fell for the same trick—I was knocking a minnowbait through the rocks under a partially blown-over cottonwood. The bait would carom off a rock and bam—fish on! Hard to find fishing like that!"

"Think so, huh? Have you forgotten everything I've ever told you about smallmouth fishing by the rocks and reefs around Waugoshance Point in northern Lake Michigan? The fishing up there is incredible. Find the boulders that are completely underwater, cast to their shady sides, and hang on or you'll lose your gear! One time I carried my wife out piggyback to one flat-topped boulder so that she could cast to a boulder in the distance, and she caught thirty-six smallmouths in a row. Did you hear me? Thirty-six!"

"I'm sure you know that each time you bring up Waugoshance to me, I get a little defensive and start messing with you. But I would actually like to try it sometime. Can I get there in less than a day?"

"Sheesh, are you ever serious? It's about three-and-one-half to four hours north of Grand Rapids, out at the west end of Wilderness State Park. You know that sometimes you drive to fishing spots farther away than that. The last few miles are on a dirt road that will twist and turn until you get a little dizzy. But overall the drive's not so bad. Once you reach the little parking area, you've got a modest hike south to the shore. But it'll all be worth it. Think you're gonna take my advice and try it soon?"

"I might give it some thought."

***

In fact, I had already done quite a bit of thinking about a trip to Waugoshance Point to try for some smallmouths. I had gone so far as to make preliminary plans for a weekend trip a few weeks in the future. I would defuse any possible objections from Wanda about spending time and money on a fishing spot I knew virtually nothing about by bringing along at least one son, in this case Jason, a little over fifteen years old. We would drive on a Friday night and stay with my brother's family at the University of Michigan Biological Station near Pellston. The next day we would drive the last twenty or twenty-five miles out to the point.

As plans sometimes do, this one started out working perfectly. Jason and I got up early that Saturday morning, drove from pavement to gravel to dirt, not a bit dizzy, and parked the van in a small area ringed by boulders big enough, probably, to stop a tank. The fact that severe thunderstorms were predicted for later in the day was on our minds hardly at all.

We used one of the boundary boulders to lay out and sort our gear and snacks. Then we packed our stuff in rucksacks and started to pull on waders. Jason was in the mood to impress, I guess, and he beat me in the silent race to get waders up and secure.

"Let's hike out the center of the peninsula for a ways," I suggested. "Then we can cut to the south, get into the water, and fish our way back toward the van."

"Fine by me," Jason was staring out the middle of the peninsula. "It looks like we might be the first ones ever to hike out that way."

"Sort of looks that way, but no way could it be true."

Not long after we headed out, it became clear that our hike was not going to be a quick one. For one thing, it wasn't the easiest walking we had ever done, making our way along a trail that in some places was muddy and in other places was hard and cobbled by fist-sized stones. For another thing, Jason kept stopping and flexing his left foot, checking whether he had somehow picked up a stone in his waders.

But the going was slow mainly because there was so much to stop and inspect. Jason noticed most things first and pointed them out to me. Snakes with delicate yellow stripes were twining through the dry husks of pencil reeds. On the edges of little sloughs we would scare up frogs, and they exploded away from us in repeating semicircles. In the sloughs we waded past some of the largest leeches either of us had ever seen; they couldn't suck through waders, we assured each other. When the sloughs grew into shallow ponds, we found ourselves walking through a fish nursery, spotting a school of inch-long perch pivoting as one here, a cluster of shiners flashing there, and then an arrow of a pike lying almost hidden above a bed of moss. Off just on the edge of our vision at one point was a great blue heron, one leg cocked in the air.

Once we thought we saw a man standing farther out on the peninsula from us, but as we got closer, we noticed he wasn't moving much. A bit later we realized that what we were seeing was really a carefully balanced stack of rocks, a kind of cairn, some gull feathers protruding from cracks and edges near the top.

From that cairn we decided to cut south to the big lake—about a quarter mile or so—and start fishing. Once we were in about three feet of water, I opted for a bronze Mepps spinner, largely because I could cover a lot of water in a short time with it. And it didn't hurt that it was close to the color of crayfish, I thought. Jason decided to use a reddish-brown tube jig. He couldn't cover as much water as fast as I, but he thought that he could more readily trigger the smallmouths by dragging the tube through the sand, leaving little trails on the bottom.

The territory we started in looked perfect for smallmouths. Shoals extended shallow to deep in rust-colored arcs, some linked to one another. And boulders were scattered around the shoals erratically.

As we approached one of these boulders, one with water around it deep enough to be green, I caught the outside edge of a boot on a rock, almost fell, but thrashed around desperately and finally regained my balance.

"Noise, Dad, noise!" Jason hissed. "Did you see the two smallmouths that you scared off? They were huge. Like submarines! They were the biggest smallmouths I've ever seen."

"Sorry. I almost went for a swim. But I'm O.K. now. Let's follow that shoal over there and see if off its edge we can find more good-looking boulders."

That shoal made for our slowest going yet. The rocks had a thin coating of some kind of algae, and it felt to me as if were trying to walk on softball-sized hailstones.

Jason broke into my cautious concentration: "Dad, look, look. There's a boulder over there—no, more to the left, there—with a bunch of small chipped-up rocks all around it. I can see the big bass lying among those rocks… time to get into some fish."

Just as he was bringing his rod into his backcast, he stopped, re-engaged his reel, and held his rod out toward me.

"Feel it."

"Feel what?"

"My rod. Here, take it in both hands."

"What about it?"

"It's vibrating. It's throbbing or something. I can even hear it. It's like it's humming."

"Huh? You're right. And my rod's vibrating too. I've never experienced anything like this. I think I'll try a cast and see if the vibrating stops."

146

As I released the line, I saw something my brain didn't want to take in. My line whirled off into the sky in lazy loops and just hung there for a second, several seconds, maybe ten seconds, until finally the weight of the lure took it down.

"What in the world?"

"Dad, I know what's going on. We learned about this in science class."

"This can't be real."

"But it is. It's some form of electricity. Can't exactly remember. Maybe static. A bunch of electricity in the air, maybe building into lightning. We've got to get out of here."

"Electricity? From where?"

The rumble from behind us answered my question. We turned simultaneously to see an enormous purple-black cloud, some kind of squall cloud, a cloud laid out like a huge roller along the surface of the water, churning and shape-shifting its way past the tip of Waugoshance Point straight toward us. Above it was a roiling mass of gray and black. To me it seemed to have intentions, and I was sure they were nasty. Suddenly a gust caught me and almost put me face-first on the rocks, and what had been a slight chop lapping against the back of our legs quickly turned into whitecaps, some with spray blown off their crests.

"You're right, Jase. We've got to move it. Let's pull our raincoats out and get them on. Then keep your rod down as low as you can. Out of the water first and then we'd better look for some kind of shelter. Try not to break an ankle along this shoal."

I don't remember exactly how we made it out of Lake Michigan, into a seeming maze of sloughs, and finally onto what seemed like continuous dry ground, bleached fragments of stone and shells and bones mixed through one another. Raindrops were hitting us. It felt like they were fired from a BB gun and every few seconds the wind got inside our rain jackets and tried to make kites out of them. The howl of the wind by itself was enough to make me wonder whether I would ever again be able to put thoughts together. Add to that the frequent thunder, with the sharp smell of ozone in the air, and I was almost frantic about getting out of there.

"Shelter," I pleaded under my breath. "We've got to find some kind of place to hide out in." And then through the streaks of rainwater on my glasses I managed to see little clusters of cedars scattered around not too far ahead of us. Some seemed no bigger than hedges gone a little wild; others were stands of cedars about as tall as they could get in such an exposed place.

"This way—quick!" I had remembered enough about shelter in a storm to pick a cluster of consistently short trees, and I scrambled under cover and held branches out of the way for Jason to crawl in after me.

If a lightning bolt were going to strike, I figured it would strike those taller cedars off to the north of us. Some wind made it through our natural shelter, but only little licks of breezes. And it was amazingly dry. I scooched around enough to make a little depression to sit in. If I could have found a large rock to lean back against, I might have been able to take a snooze.

So there we were in our little camp, feeling fairly secure from the surrounding storm. We shrugged off our rucksacks. Jason dug out his favorite candy, Laffy Taffy, and offered me some. I found my special trail mix—raisins, peanuts, and M&M's—and shared with him. He even tried a little of the green tea I had packed in a small thermos. Then we started going through some of our favorite fishing memories—memories of spuds carelessly lost through the ice, hooks accidentally embedded in relatives' shoulders and necks, and casting contests accompanied by bragging and taunting. We found new things in these stories to laugh about. And ordinarily during some of these stories we would have slapped each other on the back or punched each other on the shoulder. As it was in that cramped hiding place, all we could do was give each other little shoulder bumps.

At one point, I started on one of my favorite stories about Jason, a story featuring him as a little guy of six or seven.

"You remember that time when you caught that pike off the pier up at Les Cheneaux?"

"I remember catching perch and rock bass off the dock at Les Cheneaux Landing, bunches of them. I even got this huge dogfish once." Jason gave the dry little cough he gets when he's been in too much wind over water. "But I don't remember any pike from when I was little."

"How about this: Do you remember that one day I drove you and your brothers over to the harbor in Hessel?"

"I kinda remember that. Didn't that harbor have a bunch of floating wooden docks coming off big cement piers?"

"Yeah, and we fished off just about every one of those docks that didn't have a boat tied up to it. The neatest thing, though, was the bait we used."

"Smelt?"

"No. When we first explored the outermost cement pier, one of you guys happened to notice that there were small underwater clouds of shiner minnows in the water on the inside of it. So we rigged up a couple of our lightest poles with the smallest hooks we could find, put a speck of rolled-up bread crust from our lunch on the hooks, and then caught—or maybe snagged—half a pail-full of those shiners. Then we hooked them just under the dorsal, used the lightest bobbers we had that would suspend them, tossed them out from the end of several of those wooden docks, wedged the rods between planks, set the reel to free spool, and waited."

"Were there a couple of big cabin cruisers docked across from us?" Jason seemed to be remembering more and more clearly.

"Huge boats. Yachts. And in one of them, I remember, people were sitting out on the back deck and watching if we would catch anything. And they didn't have to wait very long. You were way down on the east end, keeping an eye on a couple of bobbers. Then you yelled out, 'Dad, dad, this bobber is three feet under the water. It's heading across toward that boat.' 'Grab the rod and yank on it!' I yelled; 'set the hook.' 'Me?' you yelled back. 'Yes, you! You're the only one over there. Set it! Set it!' So you grabbed the rod, gave a big sweeping motion, and as I got close to you, the rod started to throb. 'Help, Dad, help,' you panted; 'it's way too heavy.' 'Naw, Jase, you can get it. Just pull steady. Keep the pressure on. That's it. There you go. I've got the net ready. Bring that baby in. I think you're gonna get it. Just bring it in smooth and steady.' And then I saw this huge mass of weeds, a bushel-basket-full of weeds, and I thought, 'No, not a bunch of weeds. Not just a big pulled-out snag.'

But as you leaned back one last time and brought those weeds close enough for me to slide the net under the whole mess, I caught a glimpse of the head of a pike, and once we sorted everything out, we found that you had caught weeds and snails weighing at least twelve pounds and a northern pike weighing one or two."

"But I got it in all by myself?"

"Yup, and as I helped you release the fish, you just started to gurgle."

"That was cool. What I remember best now, though, was that the people in the cabin cruiser across the way actually stood up, came to the rail, and started to clap."

"That's when you really surprised me."

"How so?"

"Well, I'm not sure where you got it from, probably from some preschool play or something, but you very calmly put one arm behind your lower back and the other across your stomach and then you bowed across the water toward those spectators. I could hardly believe it, but you did this perfect little formal bow."

"I didn't learn it in preschool—it was in kindergarten. We had a student teacher that year who tried a writing workshop with us, and any time one of us would read to the class or show what we had drawn and the class would applaud, we were supposed to stand up and give a little bow. So it was no big deal for me to bow to those people on the boat."

"Maybe not, but they went crazy—they started to hoot and slap the railing on their boat they liked it so much. Before that I didn't know you had so much of the show-off in you."

"I really wasn't showing off. Giving a little bow just seemed like the right thing to do."

"That was really cool. But hold on a minute. The thunder seems sort of muffled. Crawl out and take a peek, will you? Maybe we can leave this hidey-hole. How does it look?"

"Just a second. O.K., it looks pretty good, Dad. All the really dark stuff is off to the east. It looks like it's even past the parking area. I think we can head out."

I made like a war-time beach invader and followed him out from under the cedar branches and was relieved to stretch out my legs.

"So what do you think?" I turned toward the water. "We've got a little time to work with yet. We could head back to the lake and make some more casts."

"I don't know, Dad. Walking all over the place in these waders is not the easiest thing I've ever done. Plus if you look out past the point you can see new thunderheads building up." He pointed.

"All right. Let's just head to the van and look for a cool restaurant for a meal. I hear there's a place called the Dam Site Inn not too far south of Pellston. Maybe we've had enough adventure for one day. You fine with that?"

"Sure. A good meal sounds great. Let's head back."

Once we were back at the parking area, we used the same flat boulder to rest our gear on as we pulled off our waders. A thunderclap from a new cell in the west got us hustling to pack our gear in the van and hit the road.

About two miles down that serpentine road, now pockmarked with puddles, I sighed and said, "Not really much of a fishing trip, was it? Sorry about that." I turned to look at Jason in the passenger seat, but he had his head slumped against the window, and he was, in fact, fast asleep.

***

So you can imagine how surprised I was—almost shocked—the next summer, when Labor Day and the fall were coming into view, that Jason found me in my downstairs office and said, "Summer's getting close to being over, Dad, and things are going to get really busy in a few weeks. Want to make another trip up to Waugoshance Point before all the commotion?"

"Huh? Are you serious? Really? Well, I guess I'm not flat-out opposed. Just pretty surprised is all. It was a fairly long drive up there and back, and last year taught us that we can't be sure in advance of the weather. But what really makes me wonder is that although we—or I guess you, really—saw some fish, we put in quite a bit of effort and didn't catch a thing. You sure you want to try again? That was about the least successful fishing trip I've ever been on."

"We'll never be able to control the weather—you've always said that. And I did see some big bass up there. But you know what? For me, the trip wasn't mainly about the fishing."

A Slow Learning of Lakes

Wanda H. Giles

When I first saw two of the Great Lakes—Ontario, followed quickly by Erie—I knew I should be overwhelmed. I come from red-clay southern Indiana, far from major bodies of water. The Great Lakes were to me a fact from geography books, like the Amazon River. At the time, tourism was rare, the industry not at all developed. But the great American road trip tradition was just beginning; and when I was a fourth grader, my father decided to take a trip to Niagara Falls. It seemed a great adventure, though my mother never developed a taste for travel; she went along, counting the days until we returned home. Having come so far and after so many years spent only in Indiana, my father was thrilled at these first views of the two Great Lakes. He was a teacher, excited to experience places he read and taught about.

But I was ten years old. In school, the Great Lakes had been drummed into our heads, partly in music class: "I got a mule / Her name is Sal / Fifteen miles on the Erie Canal. / She's a good old worker / And a good old pal / Fifteen miles on the Erie Canal." The song goes on to say how Sal and the driver have "hauled some barges in our day / Filled with lumber, coal, and hay"; they knew "every step of the way / From Albany to Buffalo." Looking back, I see that it's a fine work song, and historically evocative. But almost none of us had worked a horse or a canal; nor had we ever seen a lake. And we sang it a thousand times.

So on that trip Erie and Ontario were for me simply there. Lots of water. Part of the immense boredom of an educational childhood, taken for granted. Niagara Falls? Now, that was exciting: You could go on a boat and get wet. But I heard something, too, about energy, how the water had something to do with electricity, that sort of adult thing. Electricity itself was fairly rare in rural communities, but we had it, and as children we took it for granted; never would we have believed that Americans would overuse it; it was equally incomprehensible that our water sources could become compromised. But oddly, that one little energy fact stuck with me, and through the years I picked up a few more concepts about the utility of water. My impression then, though, was that we swam in it; we drank it; we washed dishes in it. The lakes had no life to me then. I missed a lot.

By the time I had a college degree, tourism had boomed, and I had taken many other trips. It happened one year that I went to Lake Michigan three times: on a visit to a cousin in Michigan, to an interview for a Woodrow Wilson Fellowship, and as part of a tour of Canada and New England. From those trips, I remember the summer blue of Lake Michigan at St. Joseph, the sand and grasses (it fascinated me that grasses could grow through sand; I had no idea), the wind, the serenity of the place. We stayed overnight in cabins—U.S. tourism was still young, and cabins were often literally that, a few rough clapboard buildings owned by perhaps a schoolteacher making extra money in the summer. One cabin was inconveniently high above the lake (now I would cherish a bluff like that). To get to the water, we walked down a steep, rickety wooden stairway to a rock beach. My mother was extremely unhappy on that staircase, but there at the end of it was my turning point. I had had, and loved, a course in geology. I had never realized that rocks could form beaches. Rocks were history; I had the world at my feet, brought here in part by the action of the vast water in front of me. The water was no longer just there. It defined and created everything around me. The lakes grew the East and the Midwest, and I grew into the lakes on that day in rural, lakeside Michigan.

Later in the year, fellowship in hand, I enrolled for a master's program at Northwestern University. Lake Michigan was one block from my front door on Orrington Avenue. It was quite a different lake than I had briefly viewed on trips. I remembered that when I visited in January, there was a lot of snow on the ground, some piled as high as I was tall. Having never seen anything like that before, I assumed they had just had a bad storm. I walked into the building in high-heeled shoes. But by about October of that first year of graduate school, it had become evident that high heels—or even low—were not the thing for Evanston: it was wool pants and snow boots, jackets, and blazers under heavy coats, for much of the year. And the lake: It had never occurred to me that it would change; but water, of course, has complexities, moods, transitions. It was dark blue in the fall when we listened in a glass-walled building to President Kennedy's address on the missile crisis. In the winter, in the Old English class that looked directly onto the lake, it was a gray sheet of ice, as rejecting as Old English itself, that most foreign of all the languages I have studied. I hated the lake in winter—I hated all of winter—but when I heard that the university or the city of Chicago was filling in some bit of it for more buildings, I felt a certain betrayal. And when I later heard that Erie was dying, even sometimes burning, I was horrified: How could anyone alter a fact of nature, a resource that meant and had given so much, that truly defined the central section of the country?

I wanted in my own personal life to alter the scenery—no ice, no snow—and I left for universities in California, then Texas, and never saw the lakes again for eight years. My husband was then invited to teach in an Illinois university about an hour from the lake, and during our first fall here, friends in Milwaukee had us to their house for a weekend. We viewed Lake Michigan, of course: still beautiful, still busy, still lined with cities and towns and beaches. In the following years, we've seen Lake Michigan hundreds of times. You saw it as you approached the old Goodman Theatre, as you walked on Chicago streets, as you visited Evanston for research or visits with friends. You could cruise on it, swim in it, walk or bike along it in the harmonious border of Daniel Burnham's Grant Park. You could see it from planes, as it defines both the urban and natural spaces that form Chicago's unique beauty; the view of the Lake Michigan–Chicago juncture from airplanes has always been one of my favorite travel experiences.

Wanda H. Giles

The fullness of my own Great Lakes experience, to the extent that anyone can say there is fullness concerning treasures so significant, came to me in two small moments. About ten years ago, we went to Door County, Wisconsin. On a boat trip off the peninsula, I felt the immensity of even the small stretch of water between the county and neighboring Washington Island. As on a Caribbean island looking out to sea, you could see the curve of the earth. On the water, you felt the freezing winds in the middle of August, battering your skin and reminding you of the powers that govern all living things. This was bigger than I had conceived of; this was something no one could understand from study and appreciation alone. We are human beings, privileged for a time to experience, to participate in, the world's fundamental elements.

In addition to that trip, I have always held the memory of an early visit to Lake Michigan. On that rock beach under the bluff, I had found three rocks I loved. Two were sandstone with white quartz incised into them through some distant past action; the quartz had taken the shape of a primitive animal on one, a chessboard on the other. But fine as these were, it was the smallest rock that excited me. I can see it still: a little gray rock, almost flat, hardly noticeable. But it was covered, just covered, with fossils: they were tiny little lines with clear heads, no more than an eighth of an inch long and a hair's breadth wide. I was twenty-one years old, and I was holding millennia in my right hand. The lakes are for me contained in that small rock: They are the history of this planet, the energy and the beauty and the life, including the tiniest, most enduring of lives. The majesty of a discovery like that endures; those rocks, three out of thousands or millions, spoke to me of the enduring, complex life of water and its creatures. I held the universe in my hand on that beach outside Saugatuck, grateful for my small glimpse of forever.

East

Andrew Matthew Pacton

Throughout much of my life, the Lake let me know where I stood. As I paced the labyrinths of Chicago's northwest suburbs—those minotaurean places, courts, drives—I could feel it pushing on the edge of my perception, like the rain and snow and blistering sun smashing into the cul-de-sacs themselves, necessitating a constant re-veneer of choking black asphalt to cover the thousand little cracks.

When I made my home in Milwaukee years later, the Lake continued to locate me. Near it, absurdly massive homes blotted out the sun, hiding the Lake from prying eyes. Near it, grown men would gird their loins in spandex, reflexively rage at motorists, and indulge in circuitous and furious cycling. Further away, the eclipsing mansions waned into burnt-out shambles and neighborhoods strangled by color-lines. Further away, men and women moved in slower circles, and theirs was a slower, harder rage.

***

The Lake has located me in a cardinal way, but it has also oriented me, continues to orient me: the Lake has always been east, and it has always been the path to the east.

The massive rocks that dotted a small stretch of beach in Evanston were sacred and stood upon the edge of the infinite. My fingers, crooked from lingering too long over keyboards, flex and stretch and remember the coarse faces of those great Midwestern Ma'oi, dotting the shore. At one small spot, they formed a short jetty into the waters, a cloister that clung to the shore but reached out into a slate abyss. In the dark hours, we would tremulously, reverently climb across to the very edge and settle in silently.

And pray.

In Chicagoland's perpetual twilight we made the hour's pilgrimage east, preparing ourselves through smoke and through song, through laughter and through middle-distance stares, through abstinence and through drugs. Ours was a strange ritual without a conscious beginning: we would find ourselves driving down Euclid Avenue, the suburbs melting away as we drove east, and we would know without saying that some decision had been made.

Our gridlocked souls were pulled, seduced by the Lake and its Lethean eternality, by its ability to wash away our suicidal boredom and calm our nameless restlessness. Some of us didn't make it, and the road became a little quieter.

***

Part of me wanted to probe the attraction, to analyze the pull. I was raised and trained to critique and vivisect experiences and to wrench from them some substratum, something that—even if protean—could be named and, thus, called into the sort of being I and others could understand. Maybe in the yellowing and nicotined teeth of the gas-station attendant or her hard brown eyes, I could construct the Crone. Maybe in my K-holed friend, slouched and quietly crying against the passenger-side door, whispering about all the pain that can be seen if we just look at each others' hands, I could see apotheosis.

But I resisted. I hope I still do.

Some things confound analysis or die under anesthesia. I liked—needed—the mystery. The churches we attended as children, mid-century remainders, slowly lost their patina as petrified pews and bloody saviors where replaced by ergonomic seats and abstract pastel glories. I needed the frozen mysteries of anguish, the statuary of martyrdom. I needed to see the excess to know that it was there, to know that life was not merely an orderly march to nonbeing. I needed to feel overwhelmed. I needed to be drowned by the Lake's moonlight susurrus.

It still calls to me, still lets me know where I am. The Lake itself is only seventy-five miles from my job, the same distance between my modest house and the university. As I stand before each class, I feel the waves hammer into me—pounding, shaking, eroding my position, my place—and I want to go to the Lake, want to whisper to my students, "I can't—I'm so sorry"; want to unthinkably leave, to run and scream myself hoarse; want to dive from the wave-breaking rocks and swim into the distance; want to drown in the Lake.

And I do, daily.

And I am more for it.

Andrew Matthew Pacton

The Shore

Willard Greenwood

In the parlance of my noble, crippled up father-in-law Bob, Kelleys Island is the Rock. Indeed it has a lot of rocks. Lots of rocks are continuously taken from it by quarrying, an activity that has been going on more or less uninterrupted for over a hundred years. From the air, Kelleys Island looks like a figure eight or the symbol for infinity, with two huge holes bored into it—one on the west end and one on the east end. On the ground, the magnitude of these excavations is illusory, unless you happen to be right on the quarry's edge, peering at the quarry floor hundreds of feet below.

While much of the island is developed, my in-laws' cottage is on the north shore of the Rock. It's remote and idyllic, away from the bustle of town.

I am a rabid fisherman. Bob indulges my passion. At the helm of the family Boston Whaler, Bob has ably piloted me off the north shore of Kelleys many times over the past six or so years. I envy him, because he has been fishing this bit of the shore for several decades, one of which was interrupted by four tours in Vietnam and a rather ghastly plane crash.

Hundreds of years before Bob and planes and Rolling Thunder, this island was inhabited by Native Americans. They covered a large rock on the island's south shore with pictographs that have never been translated. The untold stories on Inscription Rock have all but been erased by weather, time, and the careless feet of untold numbers of tourists. I wonder about the cosmic nature of our collective human venture and why I covet the bait shop down the shore from the disappearing pictographs.

As I wander along the narrow strip of beach Bob's family shares with three others, I realize that I don't know this stretch of Kelleys Island very well, but I love it for its constantly renewing stores of flotsam and jetsam. I have found all manner of dead fish along this sand beach and limestone shore. Millions of years ago, this beach was covered by a shallow, saltwater ocean. Every time I walk along this lakeshore, I find fossilized horn coral, gastropods, and brachiopods, rocky reminders of the shore's long history. The stench of sea grass, churned up by summer storms, and the foul odor of dead fish never stops me from picking along the shoreline for lures and carcasses. The lake has shed much of its sad modern history, but its future is constrained by its own structure and the effects of pollution. When I found a freshly dead steelhead on this stretch a few years ago, Marty told me that if I had found it ten thousand years ago, I would have eaten it. I have eaten Lake Erie steelhead, and they are not nearly as tasty as the native walleye.

The last time I fished this shoreline at night, I slid down a huge limestone slab into the water. One of my sons said, "Nice, Dad. Man 0. Wild 1." No matter. It was a warm and beautiful night. I dragged myself out of the water . . . crystal clear star-filled sky, soggy boots, lost gear. It all hinted at the persistence of the soul.

I love swimming in the shallows here. I am particularly fond of wallowing around in the water with my young sons and admiring my wife's spectacular summer tan. Her family can lay claim to knowing this part of Kelleys Island, one of the largest freshwater islands in North America. Her grandfather, an FBI agent with a prodigious talent for shotgun marksmanship, bought a humble little cottage on a secluded patch of land covered with the ubiquitous cedar tree. A generous hard-working uncle recently renovated the house into a swinging bachelor pad, complete with two beer fridges and a couple of very large flat-screen televisions. They are at home here.

The aforementioned grandfather and his wife (our boys have her eyes) are buried on Kelleys. I often carry a bar of soap and bathe in the same shallows where a man I never met, but whom my wife resembles, spent some of his last days rubbing soap in his armpits. I never met him, but we have this in common—we could not tolerate the sulphurized water in the cottage. It stank like bad eggs. When I told one of my sons that I would not let him take a bath in the sulphury egg-smelling water, he protested, "But dad, I like eggs."

This stinkiness is one of the reasons I have found myself wandering, wallowing, and looking around on this stretch of beach. I become antisocial when scouring the beach, especially if I am hunting for lures. Looking for junk and at the great things of nature, I realize I want to live for a long time. This compulsion is a misplaced hunter-gatherer instinct, one that my family encourages. I also like lingering here because this shoreline is where Beth and I first shared a few words under these same soul-affirming stars.

Occasionally, I fish with a neighbor, an obsessively precise yellow-perch fisherman, Bob Rigone, who is around eighty years old. I like the old-timers. He launches his boat all by himself. He tows it down to the shore right over there by the breakwall. In that little breakwall, lots of water snakes stop to rest and sun themselves.

On one memorable outing a couple of summers ago, I was drift-fishing in the family Whaler—it's always nice to have the motor off and be lulled by the wind and waves. Right off this stretch of shore, I lost two huge fish. Losing a large fish is the most distressing event to a dedicated fisherman, especially when the fish is unseen. Beer helps. But the beer tastes better when it's a victory beer, drunk after successfully landing a good fish.

When we're out in the boat, we're looking for walleye, the great game fish of Lake Erie. It's wonderful eating, as is its smaller counterpart the yellow perch. They are the perfect food. Wild fish is far superior to store-bought fish. Aquaculture fish are junk. I'd rather run the risk of ingesting a little mercury. Besides, a fried perch sandwich with ketchup is a delicacy.

My desire to hunt for walleye spans the seasons, but I haven't been able to indulge this pursuit. Each fall, I plan to fish for walleye at night when it's dark and the fish are congregating around the island, but something always seems to stop me. I want to partake in the specific romance of the island when summer winds down and the tourists disappear. The idea of fishing out here alone seems so perfect but I always find a reason not to do it. In the fall, I don't want to get shot by a deer hunter, or maybe it's too cold. I am busy with my tiny family and sometimes my compulsions must go unsated. I console myself with the reminder that the shore is always there.